Trail Runner's Guide

—to— Colorado

50 Great Trail Runs

Phil Mislinski, Monique Cole, and Scott Boulbol

Fulcrum Publishing
Golden, Colorado

This book is dedicated to
Samantha Cole Mislinski and Sophia Rose Baker-Boulbol,
two girls who are sure to keep us on the run for years.

This is only a guidebook. Although trail running techniques and training tips are given, it is not an instructional book on trail running or intended to be used as a substitute for the user's judgment. Trail running can be a dangerous sport, and the user of this book is ultimately responsible for his or her safety. Neither the authors nor the publisher assume responsibility for any bodily injury, damage to property, or violation of the law that may result from use of this book.

Library of Congress Cataloging-in-Publication Data
  Mislinski, Phil.
    Trail runner's guide to Colorado : 50 great trail runs / Phil Mislinski, Monique Cole, and Scott Boulbol.
      p. cm.
    Includes index.
    ISBN 1-55591-409-8 (pbk.)
    1. Running—Colorado—Guidebooks.   2. Trails—Colorado—Guidebooks.
  3. Colorado—Guidebooks.   I. Cole, Monique.   II. Boulbol, Scott   III. Title.
  GV1061.22.C6M57   1999
  796.42'09788—dc21   98–53615
                                                                                   CIP

Book design by Bill Spahr
Maps by Phil Mislinski

Cover Photos
Front cover: Dan Barger in the Leadville 100, Phil Mislinski
Back cover (inset images): Amy Beidleman running in the Colorado National Maonument (top) and near Aspen (bottom), Neal J. Beidleman.
Front and back cover background image: Rock formations at Roxborough State Park, Monique Cole.

Printed in the United States of America
0 9 8 7 6 5 4 3 2 1

Fulcrum Publishing
350 Indiana Street, Suite 350
Golden, Colorado 80401-5093
(800) 992-2908 • (303) 277-1623
website: www.fulcrum-books.com
e-mail: fulcrum@fulcrum-books.com

Contents

Foreword

I have alpine ski racing to thank for eighteen broken bones and my passion for trail running. I began running in earnest in the early 1970s while training for the upcoming ski seasons. My first real running race of any distance was a complete fiasco, if not utterly stupid. At a college party around eleven at night, a friend said that he was going to run the Denver Marathon the next morning for which he had been training. I too was training (for ski racing) and thought fast 4- to 8-mile trail runs three times a week would do just fine. I began tapering immediately by reducing my beer intake to a reasonable level until about 1:30 A.M. when I went home to carbo-load on a bowl of leftover mac 'n' cheese, a stale doughnut, and a dozen cookies. I was ready, but still not convinced I had made any real commitment. To my dismay, my friend actually did show up at 6:30 A.M., crawling through my apartment window like all my friends did during that time.

Good fortune had it that the race was full so I thought we could go home. That's when I learned the meaning of "running a race renegade." With 7,000 of my closest friends, I stormed off down the asphalt and concrete course in my disintegrating Nike Waffle Trainers. I took my usual 8-mile run pace and blazed along. By mile 20, I might as well have been wearing metal braces on my legs since my own joints barely bent anymore. I was running on youthful stupidity and pride alone. I hobbled across the finish line in 3 hours 12 minutes, curled up into a ball, and didn't walk upright for two weeks. You would think this would have cured me from distance running forever. Wrong. I liked it, but I got smarter—I adopted the "Trails Only" credo.

I began running more steadily, just for the sake of running, and almost exclusively on trails. Meanwhile, a national running craze was sweeping the country. While living in Boulder at the time, along with my close friend Kevin Cooney, I started an event that would become wildly popular … and illegal. In 1984 the first Basic Boulder Mountain Marathon was run from the doorstep of the house I rented on Spruce Street. I turned my alarm clock around in the window for the timing, we poured organic whole wheat flour across the sidewalk to form a start line, a roommate played a Jimi Hendrix version of the "Star Spangled Banner" on his electric guitar, and off we went. The "race" guaranteed the distance to be more than 20 and less than 50 miles with a "whole lot of vertical" followed by a mandatory potluck party. It lived up to its billing and then some. The true winner was the one who had completed the run and was still standing after the hours of wild dancing that broke out at the party. The BBMM became a celebration as well as a cult ritual.

The BBMM went on "officially" for 10 consecutive years until the "federales" finally shut us down. It took rangers, cops, and the city attorney, but they got us. We never obtained a single permit, permission slip, or bureaucratic approval for our event that had swelled from 22 to some 250 participants. We also never advertised, collected fees (other than for the party), or did anything materially destructive other than run on the beautiful trails and dirt roads in the Boulder Flatirons. I guess the bureaucrats had a (small) point—at 250 runners, the race was getting to be a little big. (The current allowable group size is precisely seven.) But really, the only thing the demolition of the event accomplished was to cement countless friendships among participants, make fanatical trail activists out of previously ambivalent bystanders, and galvanize what has become so important to me about running—and especially trail running—which is the personal freedom it embodies.

Few sports offer so simply the enormous freedoms and rewards that running can. Shoes, shorts, shirt, a trail heading off in some interesting direction, and you're set. I can still pack all the running gear I need for summer and winter in a small day pack. Over the years, I have run countless trail races, including numerous Pikes Peak Marathons, 50-milers, a couple Wasatch 100s, and a ton of adventure races. But they, too, are just excuses—excuses to get out by myself or with friends, to train and run on the trails. Trail running is more than just a passion. It's a remedy for anything that's wrong. It's a forum for solving the world's problems by yourself or with a group. It's an energy source for a mind and body needing nourishment. It's a celebration of motion and life.

The authors of this guide, wily veterans of many BBMMs themselves, have traveled throughout Colorado selecting a wonderful representative set of trail runs that showcase the beauty and diversity of Colorado trail running. The guide offers the right amount of information to get you there and running with the right provisions and expectations of the route. Most importantly, the book's appealing, humorous descriptions will spark your interest in exploring beyond the listed runs. The authors have made a point of not revealing all the gems, which remain for you to discover and run on your own. See you on the trails.

—*Neal J. Beidleman*

Acknowledgments

Three years of research and labor have gone into this book. We are deeply grateful to the family and friends who helped us along the way. Our little families patiently tagged along on adventures: Kathy Baker, Scott's wife, and Samantha Cole Mislinski and Sophia Rose Baker-Boulbol, our two daughters born during the process of writing this book.

Neal Beidleman, a great friend, inspired us to hit the trails in the first place and provided his spectacular photographs for the book. Neal, his wife Amy, and their daughter Nina also acted as trail guides in Aspen and Grand Junction. Several other runners, old and new friends, proved to be great regional tour guides: Matt Carpenter, Kirk Apt, Virgil Best, Rob Rysavy, and Ed Boggess. We'd also like to thank Kate Lapides for her contribution of photography and her input on responsible trail use. Paul "Hairbag" Cristina provided an invaluable "fresh eye" toward the end of the writing process, and lots of laughs on our trail runs. The great people at Boulder's Photo Craft Laboratories performed excellent processing of miles of film and provided necessary comic relief. We can't forget Tony Cash and his wonderful flying machine.

All regulars at our "Happy Hour Runs," the following runners have provided inspiration, company, the occasional free beer, and photo models: Jean-François Lamarque, Chris Meyer, Elizabeth Sulzman, Dennis "The Terminator" Coombs, Kevin Cooney, Stephanie Ehret, Peter Backwin, Ted Brown, "Uncle" Larry Dreyer, Larry "Wrong Way" Preston, Bruce Allen, Rob Chesher, Adam Chase, Anissa Dorschner, Charlie Hoffman, Jim Franklin, Jim Ham, Ellen de Money, Kay Miloshevich, Michael Maison-pierre, Kurt Blumberg, Buzz Burrell, Bruce Penner, Steve McCormick, and Norm Andrews, the original "Norm"al Guy.

We are grateful to Trails Illustrated for their generous support. And, of course, we would like to thank Daniel Forrest-Bank, our editor at Fulcrum Publishing, for his insight and respectful editing, and Bill Spahr for his great cover design and book layout.

Introduction

"Does anybody have any fooood?" I heard someone moan from 50 feet behind me as I slowly climbed up Shadow Canyon during my first marathon, the infamous Basic Boulder Mountain Marathon. Luckily for the half-starved, somewhat delirious runner behind me, I was as clueless as he, but in the opposite extreme. Not knowing what to expect on my first outing beyond 20 miles, I had brought several Power Bars and three bottles of water. I handed the guy a Power Bar as we trudged on together for the remaining climb to the summit of Bear Mountain. We've been running buddies ever since. When asked, I still insist that Scott's being a bar manager has absolutely nothing to do with why I still run with him. Everybody else points out that he doesn't really have much else going for him other than his girlish figure and a quick wit.

—Phil Mislinski

OK, I confess, Phil saved my hide on that fateful day in October 1993. It was my first marathon too, and I had no idea what to expect. Having run long distances only in road races before this, I was used to having aid stations every few miles, not to mention first-aid tents. But this was, of course, the dreaded Basic Boulder, and all I had was one 16-ounce bottle of water. Obviously I had never read a book like this before the race. I will never forget that Power Bar, or the guy who had about twenty of them, chugging along behind me (of course, Phil will tell you that I was behind him). We have been running trails together ever since, even if he does tend to hold me back a little. But his uncanny knack for embellishment is the real reason I still let him tag along. A 30-minute jog on a cinder bike path becomes a life-threatening adventure and a slight drizzle sounds like a monsoon when he tells about it. One thing is for sure, though, he knows the trails around Boulder, and all over Colorado, as well as anyone, and I'll surely be running them alongside him (or more likely in front of him) as long as my body will allow.

—Scott Boulbol

"Real Men Marry Athletes" proclaimed a T-shirt I wore to my first running date with a guy named Phil. I should have known better. He decided to see if I could walk the walk ... or run the run. I was in decent shape from backpacking and mountain biking but this was to be my first trail run up Flagstaff Trail. Now I knew nothing of the trail, but the road by the same name is the type of mountain road that makes rental car brake pads beg for mercy.

Phil promised that an abundance of switchbacks made the trail "flat." I felt like a fraternity pledge undergoing a sick initiation rite as I peered up at Phil waiting for me at the top of one grueling hill. Sure, I hiked the steeper steps, but I did not give up and, more importantly, I kept smiling. At the Flagstaff Amphitheater, I looked down at the 1,500 feet I had just climbed in less than 3 miles and thought to myself, "So that's this guy's definition of flat." I watched in awe as Phil scurried down the steep trail like a mountain goat on amphetamines. I picked my way carefully, giving in to gravity only when the trail became tamer. As the years went by, I got hooked on trail running and came to think of Flagstaff as a "flat" trail myself. I suppose Phil and I both ended up living up to my T-shirt: I became an athlete and he married me.

—*Monique Cole*

About the Book

"The road to hell is paved" proclaims a magazine ad depicting a runner on a dirt path high above the clouds in Hawaii. This sums up the philosophy of the growing number of runners who are switching from asphalt to dirt. On trails a runner can view wildlife and spectacular scenery, practice his footwork on a tricky downhill, save his joints from repetitive jarring, and maybe even have a wilderness spiritual experience. Nowhere is the movement from roads to trails more prevalent than in Colorado. After years of enjoying the adventure and camaraderie of trail running, we decided to make it easier and more fun for other people to get into our favorite sport. That is why we decided to write *Trail Runner's Guide to Colorado.*

For us trail running is much more than a sport or fitness activity. It is a lifestyle. Friday afternoons we meet a group of old and new friends to run Boulder's local trails, crack dirty jokes, and catch up on each other's lives. This end-of-the-work-week celebration called the "Happy Hour Run" always ends with cold beer and more dirty jokes and conversation. Weekends often revolve around discovering some new and beautiful part of Colorado on foot, wearing either running shoes or snowshoes. If not competing in one of the many trail races in Colorado, we are most likely on a group outing or individual adventure.

Why run instead of hike? A runner can cover more miles per hour than a hiker, thereby getting more scenery and wilderness experience for his or her time. The combination of endorphins and speed create excitement and a sense of being just another animal in the forest. Fast footwork can make downhills as fun and challenging as a mountain bike ride or a mogul ski run. And because a runner moves faster, he has a better chance of catching a glimpse of wildlife before it flees. We have seen mountain lions, black bears, a skunk, and countless deer while running in Boulder's city and county parks.

Although runners share trails with hikers, horseback riders, and mountain bikers, we need our own guidebooks. We cannot maintain a decent pace while loaded down with a backpack full of extra clothing, food, and water or when trekking up a 60-degree talus slope. Thus we need to know a trail's "runability factor" and if there are points along the way where a friend can meet us by foot, car, or mountain bike with additional supplies. We may also want to know if our favorite canine running buddy can come along or where we can apply our new talents in a trail race. These are questions that our book, the first guidebook written specifically for trail runners, answers.

Starting with a brief history of the sport, the first chapter includes many things you need to know about trail running—from technique and clothing to trail etiquette and wildlife encounters. The fifty trails themselves are organized by geographical region and cover runs for all levels, from beginners to world-class athletes. Each regional chapter opens with an introduction providing a flavor of the region, a list of resources, and "après-run" information, including places to eat, stay, and camp. An appendix with a complete list of Colorado trail races and a detailed index rounds out the book.

How to Use the Trail Write-Ups

Each trail write-up includes a map, an elevation-versus-distance plot, a topographical map for further reference, a detailed trail description, and other useful points of information as defined below.

Info Block

Each trail write-up begins with the most important trail information in a quick-read format. You will often see the word "technical" in the brief synopsis of each trail. A technical trail has challenging terrain, including roots, rocks, steps, and other obstacles. A nontechnical trail is generally smooth dirt, sand, or gravel with minimal obstacles.

Distance and Approximate Time Required

The distance of each run has been approximated to the best of our abilities using various maps and other references. All distances should be considered approximate, and they may be in error up to 10 percent in either direction. The distances quoted for out-and-back routes are round-trip. The time required is based on the time it took us to run the trail and also takes into consideration how fast The "Norm"al Guy (see page x) could complete the run. The time required will greatly depend on time of year, trail conditions, and the runner's physical ability. If you are a beginner runner or spend most of your time at sea level, be sure to expect the maximum listed time or longer.

Elevation

Starting and ending elevation, total elevation gain (number of feet climbed), high-point elevation, and low-point elevation are provided. All elevations are listed in feet instead of meters.

Best Season

Depending on the elevation, climate, and other factors, some routes are not runable in certain seasons due to snowpack, runoff, or mud. We have tried to suggest the best times of year to run each trail, but you may want to call the contact phone number listed for each trail to be sure a route is clear before traveling to the trailhead. Keep in mind that running a trail during its peak runoff time can cause severe trail damage.

Support Points

These are points at which the trail can be accessed by a car or four-wheel-drive vehicle for your friends to either set up an aid station or, if necessary, extract you from the wilderness.

Runability and Difficulty

Some trails include sections that are so steep or precarious that a runner must switch to hiking. We have included both a difficulty level (i.e., "easy" to "very difficult"), which summarizes how technical or steep a trail is, and a percentage of the run we consider "runable." A description of why a percentage of a trail is not considered "runable" is also provided. This is based on our level of fitness and running ability and the opinions of friends who have run the trails. You may end up with a different opinion. See "The 'Norm'al Guy Says" for another view on the "runability" of a given trail.

About the Trail

This section describes in brief the highlights of each trail, including views, geographic features, and history.

Trailhead Access

Specific directions on finding the trailhead from the nearest major town.

The "Norm"al Guy Says

Let's face it, not everyone is a superfit trail marathoner. For example, our friend Norm did his first run at the age of 37 and has been regretting it ever since. We decided to take one of our friends who is either a novice or nonserious trail runner on almost every run in the book. We have included their comments, quotes, moans, and pleas for help so you will have another point of view on a given trail.

Trail Description

This is where you can find the detailed descriptions on how to run a particular route. Trail names, turns at intersections, compass directions, landmarks, and approximate mileage are all included.

Alternative Routes

A detailed description of worthwhile deviations from the listed runs will occasionally be provided. If you are into doing some runs more than once, you may find our alternative routes as interesting and exciting as the main route. You should always feel free to explore for yourself. Half the fun of trail running is the adventure and discovery.

Trail Notes

This section contains miscellaneous information in a bulleted format, such as amount of foot traffic, toilet and potable water location, mountain bike access, and so on. The "Taz" Factor is also included here, with rules pertaining to dogs. (Tazman Blue is Scott's Australian shepherd and our canine running consultant.)

Natural History

The beauty of Colorado's natural areas becomes even more meaningful when you understand what you are looking at. The state has a rich and diverse natural history. In a single day, you can drive through three distinct regions, with three very different ecosystems.

Geology

Driving west across the country toward Colorado, the Great Plains seem to roll on forever. Then like a mirage in the desert, the foothills of the Front Range rise abruptly into view. Continuing west from Denver, the "Mile High" city at 5,280 feet, the mountains thrust 8,000 feet upward in only 35 miles. Farther west still, the red sandstone canyons along the Western Slope occupy the Colorado Plateau, sharing geology with the Grand Canyon and Arches National Park.

Dominating the topography of the state, and the contents of this guidebook, are the southern Rocky Mountains. Colorado has the highest peaks in the Rocky Mountain chain, with fifty-four summits over 14,000 feet high. They help form the Continental Divide, a hydrographic feature that splits the flowing waters of the continent. To the west, the rivers flow toward the Gulf of California, and to the east, the rivers flow toward the Gulf of Mexico. Also called the Great Divide, this series of peaks and ridges makes a winding, roughly north to south course through the state, providing panoramic views along the way.

Pioneers traveling west cursed the southern Rockies, which can only be crossed over passes at 9,000 feet and higher. But now trail runners pay to enter races like the Hardrock Hundred Mile Endurance Race that gains 33,008 vertical feet as the southwestern Colorado course dips and rises over 12,000 feet ten times.

The geology of the Rocky Mountains is a complex history of several hundred million years of alternating periods of uplift and volcanic activity and erosion and sedimentation. The rugged terrain at the higher elevations resulted from Ice Age activity over the past 2 million years. Glaciers carved out huge bowls, called cirques, at the heads of valleys and pockets where lakes formed. They widened valley mouths and deposited rocks on the valley floors and along ridges called moraines. Barely able to survive today's temperatures, a handful of glaciers remains along the Front Range and in Rocky Mountain National Park.

At the eastern edge of the Rocky Mountains, the peaks abruptly meet the Great Plains. Previously horizontal beds of sedimentary rock were uplifted into hogbacks, steeply tilted rock ridges as found in Roxborough State Park and the Flatirons in Boulder. The Great Plains province occupies nearly two-fifths of the state and is characterized by flat land with gently rolling hills. The plains slope downhill toward Kansas City, which is 4,000 feet lower than Denver. Between Denver and Colorado Springs, the Palmer Divide extends an arm of forest ecosystems eastward into the plains on its wide, cool highland.

The topographical relief proves less dramatic along the western side of the Rocky Mountains where they give way to the mesas of the Colorado Plateau province, some of which rise to 10,000 feet. Horizontal layers of sedimentary formations typify the tablelands of the Colorado Plateau and can be viewed like a sliced layer cake where rivers have carved deep canyons. The arid, sparsely vegetated land erodes quickly under the forces of wind and water, creating natural arches and other rock sculptures in places like Colorado National Monument.

Plants

In the plains of eastern Colorado, grass species thrive in the arid climate. Blue grama and buffalo grass dominate the grassy plains, mixed with small shrubs, flowering members of the pea and sunflower families, and taller grasses, including big bluestem, wheat grass, and June grass. In the sandy desert regions of western and southern Colorado, sagebrush dominates, along with prickly pear cactus and yucca. The aptly named scarlet paintbrush provides color in spring and can be found all the way into the tundra zone.

In the foothills of the Front Range, grasslands mix with shrublands. A variety of grasses are found here along with yucca, prickly pear cactus, sagebrush, mahogany, chokecherry, scrub oak, and junipers. Most of western Colorado's foothills are filled with the "pygmy forests" of two-needle piñon and junipers.

Rising into the forested or montane zone, you will find scattered stands of ponderosa pine, Rocky Mountain juniper, Douglas fir, and spruce. The understory is usually sparse, with wildflowers growing in sunny open meadows, including wild blue iris, three-spot mariposa lily, pasqueflowers, wild geranium, and harebells.

An abundance of wildflowers are found in the subalpine zone, marked by thicker forests. Orderly stands of pole-straight lodgepole pine are often interrupted by forests of trembling aspen or subalpine fir and Engelmann spruce. Colorado's state flower, the columbine, is often found here, along with larkspur and cinquefoil. Near treeline, gnarled limber pine trees cling to life, sometimes living longer than 1,000 years.

Above treeline is the alpine or tundra zone. Plant species including a number of sedges and herbs are usually small and low to the ground, well adapted to the cold, wet environment and short growing season. In the peak wildflower season of July, moist meadows bloom with bluebells, arctic lupine, anenomes, and scarlet paintbrush. In drier rock fields, plants form dense cushions between rocks and in cracks, including cushion phlox, one-flowered cinquefoil, moss campion, pale alpine forget-me-not, and alpine sandwort. When the high altitude leaves you breathless, take a break while admiring the many tiny, perfectly formed alpine wildflowers.

Wildlife

More than 960 species of animals roam Colorado's 25 million acres of public land with habitats ranging from short-grass prairie to alpine tundra. Best times to view wildlife are at dawn and dusk.

In the eastern plains, pronghorn antelope lope across the prairie while hawks scan for prairie dogs whose abandoned tunnels are home to burrowing owl nests. Prairie chickens dance in the early spring morning and lark buntings (Colorado's state bird) perform aerial acrobatics. Packs of coyotes are heard yipping and howling as they hunt at night in the plains and foothills. In the mountains mule deer are almost as common as squirrels, elk bugle in the fall mating season, and bighorn sheep and mountain goats cling fearlessly to steep cliffs. Above treeline, pikas chirp from the scree while chubby marmots watch humans with great curiosity and hungry greed. Ponderosa pine forests are home to a unique Rocky Mountain resident, the Aberts squirrel, recognized by its dark gray to black fur and tufted ears.

Above granite cliffs and in sandstone canyons fly small swifts that mate in midair, peregrine falcons, and golden eagles. Bald eagles, which are making a comeback nationwide, are increasing in number in Colorado. There are fourteen known nesting pairs in our state, compared to only two pairs ten years ago.

Not all wildlife sightings are positive, however. The booming growth of the Front Range and Colorado in general has increased problems between humans and wildlife. Mule deer often wander into downtown Boulder, nibbling on people's tulips and other flowers. Residents of one Denver suburb are considering trapping coyotes who have been nibbling on their pet dogs and cats. Foothills residents have to chain down their trash cans and enclose their compost piles to protect against roaming black bears. In the Weminuche Wilderness near Silverton, mountain goats hungry for the salt in human urine impose on hikers in the act.

But perhaps most disturbing of all is the increasing number of encounters between mountain lions, also called pumas or cougars, and humans. Between 1997 and 1998 three humans were attacked by mountain lions in Colorado, one fatally. The young boy was hiking ahead of his family in Rocky Mountain National Park when he was attacked. Please read the Bears and Mountain Lions sections under the Safety heading in The Basics chapter.

Chapter 1

The Basics

One of the beauties of trail running is its simplicity. Although you will face the usual backcountry dangers—changing weather, lightning, and wild animals—you can cover a lot more ground per hour running rather than hiking, so you don't have to bring as much gear. All you need are running shoes and clothes (although full-moon runs are often "clothing optional" affairs), and for longer runs, a topographical map, compass, food, and water in a hip or backpack.

Training

We have run with great 10K road runners on trails rated "moderate" in this book, and they have ended up complaining about the difficulty. Trail running is very different from road running and demands agile footwork, along with strong climbing and descending skills and strength.

On a technical trail—one with obstacles like rocks, roots, and log stairs—no two steps are the same. While this aspect makes trail running challenging, it also makes trail running fun and exciting. And if you have one leg significantly longer than the other (like Monique, or Neal Beidleman, who wrote the foreword), the constantly changing terrain can be easier on your body, compared to smooth surfaces. Trail runners in general suffer

fewer repetitive use injuries than road runners because their bodies are used differently with each step and because dirt absorbs more shock than pavement or concrete.

If you are a newcomer to trail running, you'll want to start with easier trails. That way you can gradually become accustomed to the changes in stride length, foot strike angle, and cadence required to clear the obstacles of a technical trail. It also gives you a chance to build up your ankle muscles to avoid the dreaded rolled ankle, probably the most common trail running injury. If you do strain or sprain your ankle, be sure to lay off the trails until it is completely healed. Otherwise, you will set yourself up for chronic problems (just ask Scott).

As you run, keep your upper body loose and relaxed. Let your arms swing in opposition to your feet. Breathe easily and naturally. On steep uphills, at some point you will find your stride becoming so short and slow that switching to a speed hiking pace may be more efficient. There is no shame in walking, but pushing yourself to maintain a running pace will help build your aerobic fitness and climbing strength. If you train on the same hill each week, you can set progressive goals. For example, "This week I'm going to run to that big tree, next week

I'll keep going until I reach that boulder on the right." You will be surprised at how quickly you will develop the trail running specific muscles.

On downhills try to flow over the changing terrain, touching your feet to the ground for as short a time as possible. Avoid slapping your feet down and "braking" excessively. Imagine yourself a light-footed and agile mountain goat. On technical sections, you'll want to "pick a line" by glancing 10 or more feet ahead of you and searching for the path of least resistance. Focus on the spaces between the obstacles you want to avoid, rather than the obstacles themselves. If you are staring at a 40-foot drop-off, your feet may very well follow your gaze.

Phil, the downhill pro among us, likes to perform his patented "cartoon turn" by hopping on his outside foot as he flies around a switchback on a steep downhill. Monique, on the other hand, likes to stay in control by hiking the steeper technical downhills. The trick is to run at a level at which you feel confident. If you do trip or stumble, try your best to keep your feet under you. It's amazing what you can recover from.

Although we titled this section Training, we could have called it Playing. Once trail running becomes "work" for us, we will switch to some other sport. We definitely advocate running trails for the sheer fun of it, so you can enjoy increased fitness, strength, and calorie consumption (that means we can drink more beer) as pleasant side effects. Running with friends, exploring new trails, or attending clothing-optional full-moon runs are a handful of ways to keep the sport fun.

Racing Tips

Once you have gotten addicted to trail running, racing can be a great way to take the sport to the next level. Even during races, however, we have often found a sense of camaraderie and friendly competition lacking at road races. In fact, we met several of our running buddies during trail marathons where we maintained the same pace, chatting and exchanging jokes. A list of Colorado trail races is included in the Appendix of this book.

Matt Carpenter is undeniably the world's best trail marathon runner. His VO2 max, the highest ever recorded in a runner, has helped him win eleven out of fifteen SkyMarathons (races of 26.2 miles at above 14,000 feet), including five consecutive wins in the Fila Everest SkyMarathon. He is also the course record holder of the Pikes Peak Ascent and Marathon. Below are some of his best tips for running up and down mountains. You can get more advice and philosophy at his website: http://www.skyrunner.com.

Uphills

1) To get fast on uphills, train fast on uphills.
2) Posture is everything on the uphill. Leaning forward puts too much pressure on your back. An erect posture will provide better push-off.

3) Look uphill, not at your feet.

4) On long, steep hills, switching often between hiking and running is tempting, but it makes you lose momentum.

5) Taking "baby steps" will help you maintain a good cadence when your lungs are screaming for mercy. It's like switching to granny gear on a mountain bike.

Downhills

1) Don't overstride; each landing will put extreme stress on your quadriceps.

2) Lean forward. "Running is the art of catching yourself from falling. If you lean forward, you either fall on your face or you run faster."

3) Again, as in mountain biking, you need to control your speed. Cut your stride length and increase your cadence.

4) Like a hurdler, step over, not on, rocks and other obstacles. Keep your eyes focused and level.

5) Pick as straight a line as possible down the hill. The more you move left and right, the more you increase the distance.

Equipment

Shoes are the most important item of equipment for the trail runner. Almost all running shoe manufacturers now offer at least one model of shoe designed specifically for off-road running. And while you can get started in road-running shoes, as you get more serious, you may want to purchase a true trail running shoe. Look for great fit, responsiveness, stability, and support.

Matt Carpenter's training methods must work—he was over 20 minutes ahead of the second-place runner at the 1998 Pikes Peak Marathon midway point.

Some runners prefer a higher shoe to assist in ankle support, while others prefer to strengthen their ankle muscles instead. And some runners like a hardy sole to prevent stone bruising while others (usually of lighter weight) prefer a light, flexible sole for increased "feel." Finding the perfect shoe may take some time, then the manufacturer will probably "improve" the model and you'll have to resume your search. Once you find a shoe that works for you, it may be wise to buy several pairs.

Running trails in the summer wearing only shorts (and a sports bra for women) is a delicious freedom. But for longer trails and in inclement weather, you'll want to bring along layers. Staying dry is the key to staying warm, and in Colorado's dry climate, there is often more moisture coming from a runner's body than from rain or snow. For underlayers, look for fabrics that "wick" moisture away from your skin and retain their insulating properties even when wet, such as polypropylene and polyester fleece. For outer layers such as jackets and pants, look for extremely breathable fabrics that are windproof and water resistant. It is *very* wise to bring a lightweight rain jacket on long or high-altitude runs. It may save your life.

Now you'll need a place to carry all that clothing, along with your water and high-energy foods, such as sports gels and bars. Ultimate Directions and Z-Creations are two companies that manufacture packs catering to trail runners. Some people enjoy carrying their gear in a backpack-style bag with a water bladder and handy drinking tube. Shoulder, sternum, and hip straps help keep the load stable. Other runners prefer a hip or belt pack with water bottle holsters. You'll have to experiment to see what is comfortable for you and how much carrying capacity you will need. For 1- to 2-hour runs you should be able to get by with a single water bottle belt pack with built-in pouches for food and other essentials.

The new sports gels are very handy for trail running. They are easy to eat—no chewing necessary—pack easily, and provide quick energy. These gels come in a variety of packages, including small packets, multiple-serving toothpastelike tubes, and squirt-gun tubes that fit into special holsters on your pack. But for really long runs, it's nice to bring some "real" food along. Peanut butter and jelly sandwiches, bagels with cream cheese, and heartier sports bars taste great during a rest stop.

Safety

While trail running is a relatively safe sport, there are still a number of safety concerns. Running with a companion or a group increases both the fun and safety factors. If you get injured, someone can run for help. Whether running alone or in a group, always let someone back home know where you are running and when you expect to return. Here are a few safety factors to consider.

Weather

Because Colorado is so climatologically diverse, its weather varies dramatically. If you don't like the weather in one part of the state, you can usually change it by driving into a different part of the state. The dry air makes both extremes—heat that reaches over 100 degrees and below-zero cold—more tolerable. Evenings are generally cool throughout the state, even when daytime temperatures are hot. Especially in the high country, the weather can change quickly and without warning. A sunny morning at 9,000 feet can turn into a blizzard above treeline, making hypothermia a risk and dressing for the weather a puzzle. Layers that can be added and removed depending on the weather are key.

Hypothermia

The number-one killer of outdoor recreationists, hypothermia (subnormal body temperature) is caused by exposure to the cold and is aggravated by wetness, wind, and exhaustion. Symptoms include uncontrollable shivering (that may disappear in later stages), slurred speech, incoherence, fumbling hands, a stumbling and lurching gait, and drowsiness or unconsciousness.

To prevent hypothermia, dress for the weather and bring extra clothing—a knit hat, gloves, and water-resistant windbreaker could save your life. Polyester fabrics retain more insulating properties when wet and dry faster than cotton. Avoid wind by running on the leeward side of a mountain, or protect yourself from it with windproof clothing. Stay well hydrated and fed because your body will use up its reserves quickly trying to stay warm.

To treat hypothermia, warm the victim slowly by removing wet clothing and applying a heat source such as another person's body (skin to skin in a sleeping bag), hot water bottles, or heating pads (make sure victim is protected from burns by a blanket). If the victim is conscious, you may offer warm drinks. Overly rapid rewarming, such as immersing in hot water, can cause dangerous heart rhythms.

Overheating

Overheating, while less of a risk in temperate Colorado, can still cause some serious problems. Prevention is better than treatment, so drink plenty of fluids, wear cool clothing, and try to avoid running in the peak heat of the day. Often the first indicator of a problem, heat cramps are believed to be caused by the loss of salts and fluids

resulting from heavy sweating. Severe muscle contractions in the legs and abdomen are most common. To treat cramps, rest in a cool spot while drinking cool water or a sports drink. Lightly stretch and massage the muscles.

Getting Lost

Although we have striven to provide the most accurate maps and trail directions possible in this guidebook, there is still a chance you will get lost. It is very easy to get disoriented in the wilderness, and with the maze of trails and dirt roads that covers the state, it is easy to take a wrong turn. We have indicated reference topographical maps for each trail that provide more detailed information. In unfamiliar territory, bring a topo map and compass (but learn how to use them first). We have often referenced maps from Trails Illustrated, because they are durable, accurate, and easy to read. To order, contact Trails Illustrated at P.O. Box 4357, Evergreen, CO 80437-4357; 800-962-1643; website: http://www.trailsillustrated.com.

Make mental notes of landmarks at the trailhead and at points along the way (in the Front Range, the mountains are generally to the west and the plains to the east, and rivers run west to east). When you pass trail junctions on an out-and-back route, turn around and take a quick look so you will remember the correct way on your return. And make it a habit always to pack waterproof matches—an emergency fire can both keep you warm and alert rescuers to your location.

Altitude Sickness

At higher altitudes, the atmospheric pressure is lower, therefore you get less oxygen with each breath. Runners will feel their hearts beating faster and their respiration rates increasing as they climb in altitude, especially above 8,000 feet. Air above 10,000 feet has one-third less oxygen than air at sea level. Headaches, dizziness, nausea, fatigue, lack of appetite, and difficulty sleeping are signs of altitude or mountain sickness.

The more serious pulmonary edema, a buildup of fluid in the lungs, can be deadly. Especially if you are coming from sea level, taking 2 to 3 days to acclimate to the altitude will help reduce problems. Colorado residents living at lower altitudes should train gradually for the higher runs, rather than going straight to the top of a 14,000-foot peak. If you feel the onset of mountain sickness, run slower, rest often, eat high-energy foods, drink lots of water, and if symptoms don't diminish, head to lower ground.

Lightning

A very real risk in Colorado, lightning strikes even churchgoing folk, and causes serious injuries and fatalities. Tall things attract lightning strikes, making running above treeline particularly dangerous. In Colorado, most thunderstorms occur in the afternoon, so plan on being off a mountain by 2 P.M., if possible. But morning thunderstorms also occur. Always keep an eye out for approaching storms and head for lower ground if you see one coming. If you get caught in a thunderstorm in the mountains, avoid hilltops, ridges, open areas, lone trees, shallow caves, and the base or edge of a cliff. Try to crouch down in a ravine or drainage (don't sit in water, though), in a deep, thick cave, in a forest, or between rocks in a boulder field. If you are caught above timberline, sit on a small rock hugging your knees and place insulating material (a jacket or pack) under you, with only your feet and butt touching the ground. Individuals in a group should stay several yards apart.

Sunburn

A thinner atmosphere at high altitudes also means the sun's ultraviolet light is more intense. And don't be fooled by the "shade" of clouds—those UV rays pass right through. Also beware of snow's reflective quality, which intensifies the sun's burning effects. To beat the sun, slather on the sunscreen and wear a hat and sunglasses.

Giardia

The single-cell parasite called giardia lamblia lives in stream and lake water. Even those temptingly cool high-mountain streams are suspect. The invisible protozoan can survive temperatures as low as 40°F and is spread by the excrement of a variety of animals, including squirrels, marmots, beaver, elk, cattle, dogs, and especially people. One bout of the resulting cramps and diarrhea that set in within 1 or 2 days, and you'll never drink unfiltered water again. Hopefully, you'll heed this warning and skip even the single bout. Carry enough water with you or bring along iodine tablets or a water purifier (remember that this only helps if you are running near a water source). Handy new filters that fit inside a water bottle and remove giardia as you drink are now available in outdoor stores.

Hunters

Hunting is allowed in natural areas managed by the U.S. Forest Service, Colorado Division of Wildlife, Bureau of Land Management, and State Parks Division. Trigger-happy hunters have been known to fire at other humans, mistaking them as prey. As the hunting seasons vary by region (most hunting is in the fall), it's best to call the contact number listed for each trail to get specific dates or contact the Colorado Division of Wildlife at 303-297-1192. If you know there are hunters in the area, wear bright clothing, run with someone else, and carry on a conversation. If alone, talk or sing while running so the hunters know you're human, and never trail run while listening to headphones.

Bears

Black bears are fairly common in Colorado, even in the Front Range foothills. Fortunately, wild bears rarely attack people unless they feel threatened or provoked (especially a mother protecting her cubs). To avoid an encounter with bears, talk or sing on the trail to prevent surprising them. If you do see a bear, do the following:

- Calmly walk away if it has not seen you.
- If it has, stop and back away slowly while facing the bear.
- Give a bear plenty of room to escape.
- Speak softly and try not to show fear.
- If a bear rears up on its hind legs, don't panic; it may just be sniffing the air to identify you.
- A bear may try to intimidate you by charging to within a few feet, then withdrawing.
- If a bear does attack, fight back. Bears and lions have been effectively driven away with rocks, sticks, binoculars, and even bare hands.

Mountain Lions

Two people have been killed by mountain lions in recorded Colorado history; many more have been attacked. The first fatality was in January of 1991, when an 18-year-old student was killed while running near Idaho Springs. More recently, a 10-year-old boy was killed in July 1997 in Rocky Mountain National Park. Runners are particularly at risk because running apparently stimulates a lion's instinct to attack. Follow the above bear recommendations and do everything you can to appear larger—raise your arms and open your jacket. If the lion behaves aggressively, throw stones, branches, or anything within reach—without crouching down or turning your back.

Backcountry Ethics

The beautiful natural areas we enjoy while trail running can only be preserved by responsible travel and camping. You may also want to invest a little sweat equity in your favorite trails by

Trail running model Chris Meyer shows that getting muddy can be fun. Hair and makeup by Jean-François Lamarque.

volunteering for a day of trail building or maintenance. Aside from meeting other fun people and easing your conscience, you will also learn a lot about erosion and the effects of human use on trails. Volunteers for Outdoor Colorado manages a clearinghouse of trail work projects organized by a variety of mountain bike and other outdoor advocacy groups. They can be reached at 303-715-1010.

The following guidelines have been adapted from materials provided by Leave No Trace, Inc., a nonprofit organization that promotes responsible outdoor recreation. For more detailed information, contact LNT at P.O. Box 997, Boulder, CO 80306; 303-442-8222 or visit their website at http://www.lnt.org.

Running

- Stay on designated trails.
- In remote, trail-less areas, travel on durable surfaces such as snow, rock, sand, and pine needles.
- Avoid areas that are marked "sensitive" or "closed for revegetation."
- Do not cut switchbacks or make shortcuts.
- Use hard-surfaced paths and/or step stones during wet conditions.
- Using trails during spring runoff can cause severe erosion—try to avoid wet trails.
- If you do encounter mud or snow on trails, don't create new trails to avoid getting messy (some people pay top dollar for mud baths; trail runners get them for free).
- Respect other users: Yield to hikers and don't startle them from behind.
- Step to the downhill side of the trail and talk softly when encountering horses and other pack stock.
- Never feed or chase wildlife.
- Avoid trampling vegetation and don't take flowers, pinecones, or other plants.
- Carry out all trash; be careful not to accidentally drop food wrappers.

Dogs

- Follow the regulations of the area you are visiting.
- Don't allow your dog to chase wildlife.
- If your dog is unreliable, use a leash on "voice and sight control" trails.

- Even if your dog is reliable, it is a good idea to bring a leash for use near trailheads or in areas of high traffic.
- Clean up waste in plastic bags. Tip: Make Fido carry it out in a dog pack.
- Keep dogs on leash in bear country.

Camping

- Choose an established campsite in popular areas; spread use in remote areas.
- Camp at least 200 feet away from trails and water.
- Restrict activities to the area where vegetation is compacted or absent.
- Don't "clean" sites of leaves and needles; this organic litter helps prevent erosion and trampling.
- Choose a site large enough for your group. Don't enlarge a site or create "satellite" sites.
- Hang your food at least a few feet off the ground.

- Pack out all trash and garbage, including food particles strained from dishwater.
- Use stoves instead of fires (in some areas fires are strictly prohibited).
- Properly dispose of human waste (check local regulations and recommendations).
- Pack out toilet paper and feminine products in plastic bags.

Camping in Bear Country

- Separate sleeping, cooking, and food-hanging sites by at least 100 feet.
- Prepare food downwind of campsite.
- If you see signs of bear activity at a site, move on.
- Hang food, toiletries, and garbage at least 12 feet off the ground and 4 feet away from tree trunks.
- Don't burn or bury garbage; instead double-bag it and hang it with food.
- Avoid leftovers—cooked food has a strong scent.

Chapter 2
Denver & Golden

The rock formations near Denver provide unique terrain for trail running.

In recent years, economic indicators and business magazines have pointed toward Denver as one of the best places to live in the country. It has all the attractions of other big cities—art and history museums, professional sports teams, an ethnically diverse population, and a historic downtown, "Lodo," filled with cafes and galleries. But it also lies within a short drive of the best ski areas and forests in the Rocky Mountains. All this in a relatively mild climate with more than 300 days of sunshine per year.

As a result of its allure, the metro area is bursting with new development. Planned communities pop up almost overnight where once there was only prairie or farmland. Denver acts as a transportation and commercial center of the Rocky Mountains and is the largest metropolis within a 600-mile radius. Still, it is not difficult to escape the city.

Denverites are fanatic outdoor recreationists—fly fishermen, rock climbers, mountain bikers, backpackers, skiers, and, of course, runners. A great example of taxpayers' dollars being put to good use, the Jefferson County Open Space includes approximately 30,000 acres of land acquired and developed with revenue from a local one-half of 1 percent sales tax. These parks are filled with well-maintained multiple-use trails throughout the foothills west of Denver. Many of these parks are close to Golden, best known as the home of the Coors Brewery, and Morrison, a quiet Victorian small town. The parks are home to bear, mountain lions, deer, coyotes, red foxes, golden eagles, and other wildlife.

Jeffco sometimes closes trails in its Open Space parks to protect nesting raptors and to prevent erosion when conditions are muddy. To avoid a useless drive to the trailhead, especially during early spring or after a heavy rain, call the trails hotline at 303-271-5975.

In addition, a number of city parks and state parks and recreation areas ring the metro area, including Roxborough, Cherry Creek Lake, Bear Creek Lake, and Chatfield Lake. Farther to the west and south, the Pike National Forest offers more recreational opportunities. Denver's mile-high altitude makes it a great place for lowlanders to acclimate before heading to the higher reaches of the Rockies.

Even back in its beginnings during the mining days, Denver acted as a gateway to the mountains. In 1858 gold dust was discovered in the Platte River near present-day Englewood. Even though the gold soon panned out, rumors spread east of a big strike and Denver soon was flooded with would-be millionaires. After a truly big strike was made in Central City the next year, Denver became a supply station for miners headed west into the mountains.

The Denver Pacific Railroad, finished in 1870, followed closely by the Kansas Pacific, guaranteed Denver's importance as a supply hub for the mining towns and the quickly growing ranching and farming communities of Colorado. And the richest of the miners, ranchers, and farmers built grandiose mansions in the city's center. But all the grandeur and wealth couldn't kill Denver's reputation as a rowdy Wild West town.

In the 1890s the price of silver fell, almost destroying Denver's economy. Under the leadership of Mayor Robert Speer, the city was spruced up with better infrastructure, classy parks, and no brothels. Denver began to look toward tourism and agriculture to diversify its industry. Over the last century, Denver has seen its shares of ups and downs, but the present boom has no end in sight.

Après-Run

There's always a crowd at the Denver Chop House & Brewery, especially when the Rockies are playing at nearby Coors Field. Hearty food and a long list of brews are served in the old Union Pacific Railroad's "Head House." A huge number of brew pubs, restaurants, and bars are located in LoDo. If you're really hungry after a trail run and can't make it to downtown, try the Morrison Inn in the middle of Morrison's main street for creative, if not authentic, Mexican food.

There are so many places to stay in Denver, we can't even begin to list them. All the major chains have hotels here and there are a number of historic inns and hotels as well. The Brown Palace Hotel was built in 1892 during Denver's heyday with Colorado red granite and Arizona sandstone gracing its Victorian exterior (303-297-3111 or 800-321-2599). Even if you don't stay there, you can enjoy their elegant afternoon tea (don't show up in your running clothes) or delicious Sunday brunch. You may want to consider staying farther west, in Golden, Morrison, Evergreen, or Conifer, for example, to be closer to the mountain parks. For information on accommodations, contact the Convention and Visitor's Bureau (see below).

You can actually camp within Metro Denver, if you are so inclined. In Lakewood the Indian Paintbrush Campground in Bear Creek Lake Park has fifty-two campsites, some with electric hookups, and some can be reserved by calling 303-697-6159. Backcountry camping is allowed, by permit only, in the White Ranch and Reynolds Parks (see Jefferson County Open Space below). Farther west, about

45 minutes from Denver, many campsites are available in Golden Gate Canyon State Park (call 303-582-3707 for reservations).

Resources

Denver Metro Convention and Visitor's Bureau, 1555 California Street, Denver, CO 80202; 303-892-1112; website: http://www.denver.org

Jefferson County Open Space, 700 Jefferson County Parkway, Suite 100, Golden, CO 80401; 303-271-5925

Roxborough State Park, 4751 N. Roxborough Drive; Littleton, CO 80125; 303-973-3959

Pike National Forest, South Platte Ranger District, 19316 Goddard Ranch Court, Morrison, CO 80465; 303-275-5610

Bergen Peak Loop

—Scott Boulbol

A combination of wide single-track trails climbing gradual switchbacks to the top of Bergen Peak near Evergreen.

Time: 1.45–2.5 hours
Distance: 13.5 miles
Start & End Elevation: 7,950 feet
Total Elevation Gain: 1,820 feet
High Point: 9,500 feet
Low Point: 7,870 feet
Best Season: Spring to late fall
Support Points: None
Runability: 100%
Difficulty: Moderate
Type: Lollipop loop
Map: "Elk Meadow Park Map," Jefferson County Open Space
Contact: Jefferson County Open Space, 303-271-5925

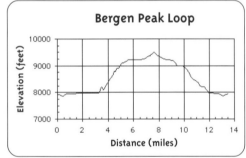

About the Trail

If you are looking for a test run to judge the kind of shape you are in, this is a great loop allowing runners to really push their limits. There is even a race here every fall, called the Bergen Peak Trail Race, that takes a slightly different route, but provides some great competition and a personal challenge. On our route, the climbs are just steep enough to maintain a decent pace, but they seem to go on forever. The smooth sandy trails make for a slightly slippery surface. While this won't slow the pace on the uphill, it does make for a

Bergen Peak Loop

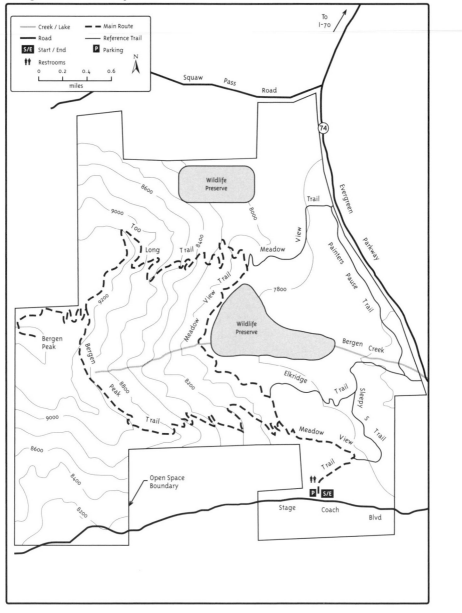

precarious downhill. Still, I enjoyed the descent immensely, finding myself wishing I had worn gloves, so I wouldn't rip up my hands while swinging around the trees at each switchback. Elk Meadow Park, where this run starts and ends, has many miles of beautiful and diverse trails to run. You can find anything from a steep mountain climb to a casual romp through rolling meadows. We recommend you try these trails on a mountain bike as well. They

Wildflowers and pine trees line much of the Bergen Peak Trail. Photo by Scott Boulbol.

> ### The "Norm"al Guy Says
> "They should call this climb the 'Too Long Trail' ... What? Oh, they already do? Well, I see why!"

are allowed on all trails in the park. Due to the heavy bike traffic, however, we recommend you run or ride here only on weekdays, or very early on weekends.

Trailhead Access
From Denver, head west on I-70, then south on Hwy. 470 and west on Hwy. 74 toward Evergreen. From Evergreen, continue west (northwest) on Hwy. 74 about 2 miles to Stagecoach Boulevard and make a left. Go west about 1.25 miles to the Elk Meadow Park parking lot on the north side of the road.

Trail Description
From the parking lot take the Meadow View Trail about 0.3 mile until it veers left and heads west, past the Sleepy "S" Trail intersection. Stay on Meadow View Trail about 2 more miles as it rolls to the north. Make a left onto the Too

Long Trail, and start to climb. About 2.5 miles up, there will be an intersection with the Bergen Peak Trail. Turn right and climb a mile to the summit. Turn around and descend 1 mile back to the intersection and turn right, continuing on the Bergen Peak Trail for about 2.7 miles down to the Meadow View Trail. Turn right and take this about 1 mile back to the parking lot.

Alternative Route
To follow the route of the race, turn right at about 0.3 mile onto the Sleepy "S" Trail, and follow it about 1.1 miles to the Painters Pause Trail. Turn left and go about 1 mile to the Meadow View Trail. Turn left again and take this about 1 mile to the Too Long Trail. Turn right here and follow above directions back to the start.

Trail Notes
• Heavy foot and bike traffic, especially on weekends
• Dogs allowed on a leash
• Bathrooms at start
• Bikes allowed
• No fee charged

Buffalo Creek–Colorado Trail

—Phil Mislinski

A rolling, smooth single track through ponderosa and lodgepole pine forest with frequent views of major rock formations.

Time: 3.0–4.0 hours
Distance: 17.4 miles
Start & End Elevation: 7,640 feet
Total Elevation Gain: 1,880 feet
High Point: 8,080 feet
Low Point: 7,400 feet
Best Season: Spring through fall
Support Points: Forest Access
   Road 543 crossing
Runability: 100%
Difficulty: Easy
Type: Out-and-back
Map: Trails Illustrated Number 135
Contact: Pike National Forest, South Platte Ranger District, 303-275-5610

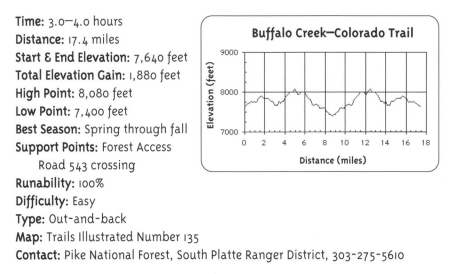

About the Trail

This is not the start of the Colorado Trail from the Denver side, but this is where it really starts to get good. This section of the Colorado Trail provides the ideal place for a scenic and relatively easy, long training run. With only 1,880 feet of elevation gain over the recommended 17.4 miles, this run is virtually flat. Unlike many flat runs, this one is far from boring. The smooth winding single track through dense forests will keep your mind awake. The occasional short climbs to the ridge tops provide the opportunity for interval training as well as great views of rock formations and the gentle mountains covered in pine trees. During spring and early summer, wildflowers line the trail and fill the many small meadows along the way.

Trailhead Access

Take Hwy. 285 south from Denver to Conifer. Continue on 285 south 6.6 miles to Pine Junction and turn left on Pine Valley Road. Turn right into the parking area for the Buffalo Creek Recreation Area after 13.3 miles.

Trail Description

On this out-and-back on one of Colorado's best-known trails it is nearly impossible to get lost. From the parking lot, head west on the trail that is marked only with an arrow. After approximately 1.5 miles, cross Road 550.

Buffalo Creek—Colorado Trail

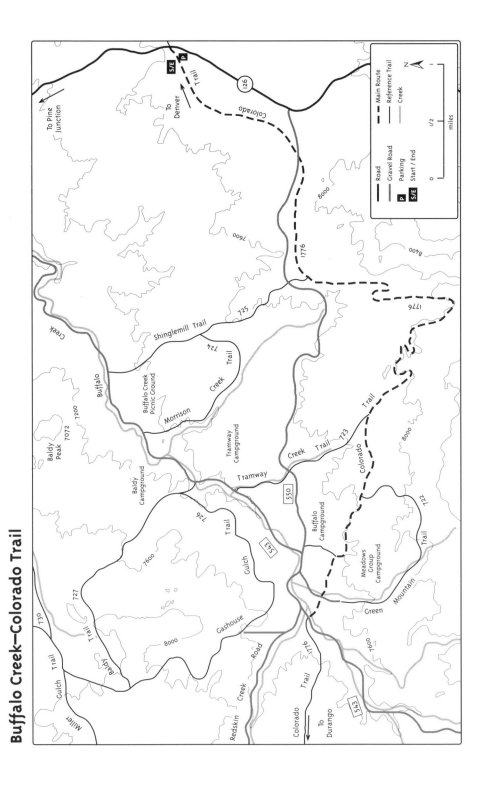

The "Norm"al Guy Says

"I can't believe that I just ran over 17 miles without an out-of-body experience."

Follow the trail as it winds south, then west. Cross Road 550 a second time and continue 0.25 mile to Road 543. Turn around here or continue on as far as Durango. *Note:* There are small creeks at the second Road 550 crossing and the Road 543 crossing.

Alternative Route

If you want to add about a mile on your way back, turn right at the first road crossing and pick up the Green Mountain Trail (722) after 0.25 mile. Follow this trail as it loops east then north back to the Colorado Trail. Turn right on the Colorado Trail and continue back to the parking lot.

Phil Mislinski heads toward Durango on the Colorado Trail near Buffalo Creek. Photo by Monique Cole.

Trail Notes

• Moderate to high bike traffic on the weekend
• Dogs must be under voice and sight control at all times (a leash is recommended)
• No facilities
• No potable water
• No fee charged

Mount Falcon

—Phil Mislinski

This run covers a wide variety of terrain from smooth, wide path to steep, fairly technical single track. Spectacular views of Red Rocks Park, the Continental Divide, and downtown Denver can be seen from several points along the run.

Time: 1.75–3.0 hours
Distance: 12 miles
Start & End Elevation: 6,310 feet
Total Elevation Gain: 2,480 feet
High Point: 7,650 feet
Low Point: 6,310 feet
Best Season: Year-round
Support Points: Mount Falcon
   Open Space West Entrance
Runability: 90–100%
Difficulty: Moderate
Type: Lollipop loop
Map: "Mount Falcon Park Map," Jefferson County Open Space
Contact: Jefferson County Open Space, 303-271-5925

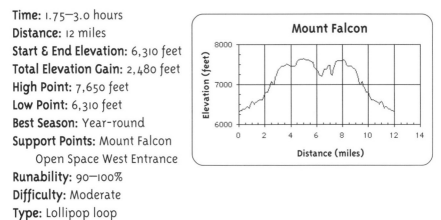

About the Trail

Starting with a long, steady climb to the Walker's Dream Shelter up fairly rough single track, this is a classic foothills run. With every switchback you get better views of the plains to the east and the foothills to the north and south. What makes this climb exceptional are the views of Red Rocks Park to the north. If you have ever seen a concert at Red Rocks you will appreciate this view. Once reaching the crest at Walker's Dream Shelter, you will begin to pass through meadows that are covered in wildflowers for much of the spring and early summer. The groomed walking trail may seem boring at this point, but the gentle rolling of the terrain and the occasional views of the Continental Divide more than make up for it. Enjoy the views and easy running because upon reaching the Parmalee Trail, just running will absorb most of your attention for a while as you descend the steep single track into the trees. Once looping back around on the Parmalee Trail, you can get some bonus miles and views by heading up the Tower Trail for a quick loop, or you start heading back to the parking lot on the Meadow Trail.

Trailhead Access

From Denver, head west on I-70 and take the Hwy. 40 exit to Morrison.

Mount Falcon

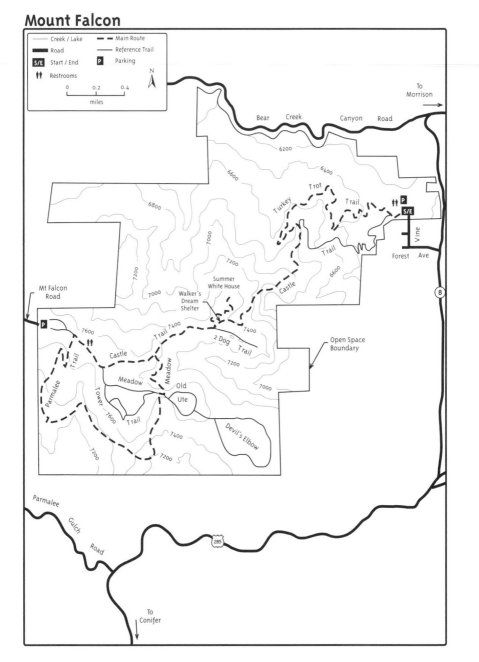

Take Hwy. 8 south out of Morrison. After approximately 1 mile turn right on Forest Avenue. Turn right on Vine Street after one block and follow Vine into the East Mt. Falcon parking area.

If you have a support vehicle meeting you at the west parking area, they should drive south on Hwy. 8 past the east parking area, then head west on Hwy. 285 toward Conifer. Before reaching Conifer, a right turn on Parmalee Gulch Road, then a right on Mt. Falcon Road, will take them to the west parking area.

Trail Description

From the parking lot, head west on the Castle Trail and immediately turn right onto the Turkey Trot Trail (this is a much nicer climb and it is closed to bikes and horses). Follow the switchbacking trail until it rejoins Castle Trail after approximately 1.7 miles. Turn right on Castle Trail and continue until you reach the Walker's Dream Shelter. A worthwhile diversion is to head north for 0.4 mile to the Summer White House Ruins for a quick out-and-back and spectacular views of the divide. After the out-and-back, head west on the Castle Trail veering right at the next two intersections until you reach the Parmalee Trail intersection near the west parking area. Head south on the Parmalee Trail and follow the single track as it winds around the southern edge of the summit until you reach the intersection with the Meadow Trail and Tower Trail. Turn right on the Meadow Trail and then left after 60 yards to stay on the Meadow Trail. Turn right (northeast) at the intersection with the Castle Trail and follow it back to the Turkey Trot Trail. Take the Turkey Trot Trail or the smoother, but just as steep, Castle Trail back to the parking area.

> ### The "Norm"al Guy Says
>
> "I'm glad that I brought lots of water because the long, hot climb at the start was about to make my head explode."

Alternative Route

From the Parmalee, Meadow, and Tower Trails intersection, head west on the Tower Trail to reach the Tower and true summit. Continue past the Tower until you intersect with the Meadow Trail. Turn right (southeast) on the Meadow Trail and follow it back to the intersection with the Parmalee Trail. Use the directions in the Trail Description to get back to the parking area. If your legs are feeling good, this is a very worthwhile add-on loop.

Trail Notes

- Light horse traffic
- Moderate bike traffic: Bikes must yield to all other trail users. Pay attention because there are several blind corners on this route
- Outhouses at both the east and west parking areas
- Bikes and horses are not allowed on the Turkey Trot Trail
- Dogs must be on a leash unless posted otherwise. (In those areas they must be under voice and sight control at all times)
- No fee charged

Roxborough State Park

—Monique Cole

This jewel of a park close to Littleton is a naturalist's nirvana. A dramatic variety of geology, flora, and fauna can be experienced on these two loops that connect into a figure eight with gentle to moderate hills on a wide gravel path and narrow single track.

Time: 40–60 minutes

Distance: 4.9 miles

Start & End Elevation: 6,180 feet

Total Elevation Gain: 652 feet

High Point: 6,460 feet

Low Point: 3,028 feet

Best Season: Year-round

Support Points: Visitor's Center

Runability: 100%

Difficulty: Easy

Type: Loop

Map: Trails Illustrated Number 135

Contact: Roxborough State Park, 303-973-3959

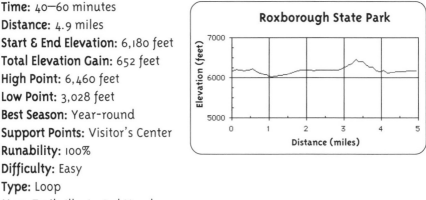

About the Trail

Roxborough is the first of Colorado's state parks to be designated both a Colorado Natural Area and a National Natural Landmark. While the park's restrictions are numerous (no rock climbing, pets, or mountain bikes allowed), their purpose soon becomes obvious. Roxborough looks like a miniature version of Garden of the Gods, only with hordes of wildlife, instead of RV-driving tourists. Scrub jays, meadowlarks, and warblers perch atop the flower spikes of the mullein plant while rufous-sided towhee birds scratch the ground below the scrub oak and chokecherry shrubs. The feeders at the Visitor's Center attract dive-bombing hummingbirds

Geology and ecology run wild in Roxborough State Park. Photo by Monique Cole.

Roxborough State Park

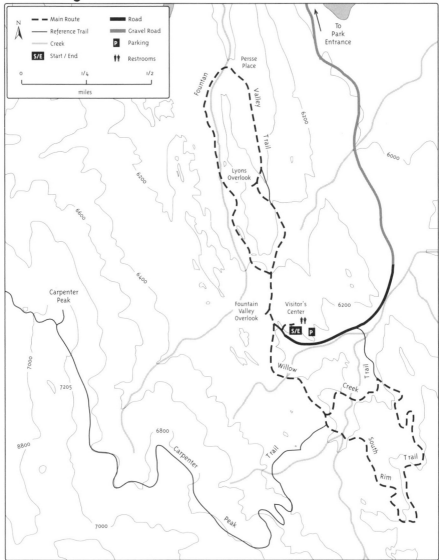

> ### The "Norm"al Guy Says
> "This route is easy enough to enjoy the great views along the way."

while golden eagles prefer to perch in the occasional ponderosa pine or soar over the sandstone hogbacks hunting for rattlesnakes, pocket gophers, meadow voles, and rock squirrels. An occasional fur-filled dropping is sign of a coyote passing through, but runners should be particularly conscious of the mountain lions that roam the park. Mid-April to mid-June is the best time to enjoy the grand array of wildflowers in the park. Butterflies and other insects flutter by, with binocular-armed amateur entomologists in hot pursuit. In fall, the park's dominant scrub oak leaves are ablaze with color. In midsummer, radiant heat from the rock formations will make you want to run in early morning or late evening—or just sit on one of the many shady benches beside the trail. And in winter the park is a paradise for cross-country skiers and snowshoers.

Trailhead Access

From Denver, head south on Hwy. 85 (Santa Fe Drive) to Titan Road. Turn right (west) and continue 3.5 miles, then turn left to stay on Titan Road. After another 3 miles a sign will mark the entrance to Roxborough State Park.

Trail Description

Start your run a few steps north of the Visitor's Center on the Fountain Valley Loop, a wide gravel path with gentle grades that make it accessible to wheelchairs. Pass by the Fountain Valley Overlook Trail on your left, then take the right fork to run the loop counterclockwise. The trail runs roughly north, with the dramatic Fountain Formation sandstone fins on the left. Take a left turn at the sign indicating Lyons Overlook, where a short single-track trail climbs to a dramatic view of the park. Leaving the overlook, take the left fork to return to the Fountain Valley Loop. The trail continues north, then turns southwest at a small turn-of-the-century cottage. At trail marker 12, see if you can find George Washington's profile (with his nose pointing to the sky) in the large red rock formation across the meadow. Continue heading south to return to the Visitor's Center. A few steps southwest will take you to the start of the South Rim Loop, a narrower, shadier, less traveled, and slightly steeper and more rugged trail. Run southeast past the junctions with Carpenter's Peak and Willow Trails. With a handful of switchbacks, the trail climbs past some stately Douglas fir trees that beckon you into their shade. Then the trail turns east and north to follow a ridge with great views of Fountain Valley. After a short, switchback-ing descent, take a left turn onto the Willow Trail to avoid running a half-mile of pavement. The Willow Trail crosses the small valley (southwest) and rejoins the South Rim Trail where a right turn will take you back to the Visitor's Center.

Alternative Routes

A right turn off of the South Rim Trail will take you to the top of Carpenter Peak, the highest point in the park. Farther along the same trail, you can meet up with the Colorado Trail.

Trail Notes

- Moderate to high foot traffic on spring and fall weekends
- No horses, dogs, or mountain bikes allowed
- Toilets and potable water at the Visitor's Center
- No hunting
- State parks admission fee

Three Sisters and Evergreen Mountain

—Scott Boulbol

This figure-eight loop combines the best of Evergreen's geological landmarks. The mostly single-track trails roll past towering rock formations and offer magnificent views of Mt. Evans and the Continental Divide.

Time: 1.5–2.0 hours
Distance: 10 miles
Start & End Elevation: 7,700 feet
Total Elevation Gain: 1,580 feet
High Point: 8,450 feet
Low Point: 7,400 feet
Best Season: Spring through fall
Support Points: Three Sisters
Parking Area
Runability: 100%
Difficulty: Moderate
Type: Figure-eight loop
Map: "Alderfer/Three Sisters Park Map," Jefferson County Open Space
Contact: Jefferson County Open Space, 303-271-5925

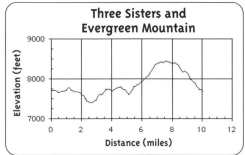

Scott and Taz Boulbol scamper along the top of the Brother. Photo by Jean-François Lamarque.

About the Trail

We originally set out to find a trail closer to Denver, but this system was so beautiful and perfect for running we had to include it. The route passes the geological highlights of Jefferson County's Alderfer/Three Sisters Park just west of Evergreen. The first section of this loop offers a relaxing but very beautiful loop in and around the Three Sisters and the Brother rock formations. Serving as landmarks for Evergreen residents since the pioneer days, the rock outcrops are formed of beautiful silver plume quartz, a metamorphic rock from the Precambrian Era. This is a rolling section, with scenic turnouts around every bend. There

Three Sisters and Evergreen Mountain

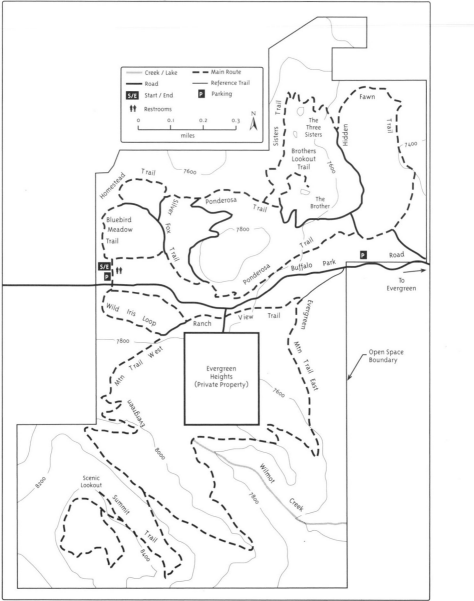

is some climbing, but the smooth, graded trail makes these a perfect warm-up, not a burnout. At the end of this first loop, a trail leads across the street to the Evergreen Mountain Trail, and the fun really begins. This is a steady climb

The "Norm"al Guy Says

"Those are the friendliest sisters I've chased after since the Lovejoy triplets."

up to the summit, but is again very smooth and well graded all the way up, and the views at the top are well worth the effort. A scenic loop around the summit offers just rewards, along with the potentially crazy downhill.

Trailhead Access

From Denver take I-70 west to the Evergreen exit (Hwy. 74). Take Hwy. 74 south to Evergreen and veer right onto Hwy. 73 south. Make another right onto Buffalo Park Road and head west. Pass the first parking area for Alderfer, and continue to the second one. Turn right and park.

Trail Description

From the west parking lot, take the Bluebird Meadow Trail north to the Homestead Trail. Turn left and run to the Silver Fox Trail. Turn left again for about 0.1 mile and this leads to the Ponderosa Trail. To get to the top of the Brother, continue straight east on Ponderosa to the Brothers Lookout Trail and go left. The summit is about 0.2 mile up. Return to the Ponderosa Trail and go right. After about 0.1 mile, make a right on the Three Sisters Trail. This leads up and over the Three Sisters rock formations, and down switchbacks on the other side. Turn left at the bottom onto the Hidden Fawn Trail. After about 0.7 mile, this trail feeds into the south side of the Ponderosa Trail. Continue west about 0.7 mile to the Silver Fox Trail, make a left and look for the Bluebird Meadow trail on the left. Take this 0.2 mile back to the parking area and turn left, cross the street, and turn left again onto the Wild Iris Loop Trail. Take this trail across the meadow and turn left onto the Ranch View Trail. This starts to descend, crosses a street, and continues down to the intersection with the Evergreen Mountain Trail East. Turn right onto Evergreen Mountain Trail East and continue all the way up the mountain. Near the top, take the Summit Trail, on the left, to reach the top, and circle the summit counter-clockwise. Return down the Summit Trail and stay left at the intersection onto the Evergreen Mountain Trail West. This leads down the mountain to the Wild Iris Loop Trail at the bottom. Turn left and cross the meadow back to the parking area.

Alternative Routes

Either of these individual loops makes a great short to medium run. Simply follow the directions from the parking lot.

Trail Notes

- Moderate to heavy foot traffic
- Dogs allowed on a leash
- Bathrooms at parking lot
- Bikes allowed
- No fee charged

White Ranch

—Scott Boulbol

A hilly single-track and dirt road loop around the perimeter of White Ranch Park with challenging climbs and descents and long rolling sections with gorgeous views of the mesas and buttes around Golden.

Time: 2.5–3.5 hours
Distance: 17.6 miles
Start & End Elevation: 6,600 feet
Total Elevation Gain: 3,170 feet
High Point: 7,840
Low Point: 6,380
Best Season: Year-round
Support Points: None
Runability: 90–100%
Difficulty: Moderate to difficult
Type: Loop
Map: "White Ranch Park Map," Jefferson County Open Space
Contact: Jefferson County Open Space, 303-271-5925

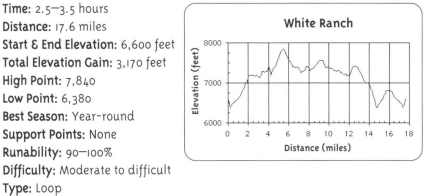

About the Trail

Though we chose to run the perimeter loop at this park (When have we ever been known to take the short route?), there are ample trails here for various runs. One thing remains constant, however—they are all hilly and some are quite challenging. The perimeter loop starts off with a long steady climb to the top of the mesa and then rolls considerably the rest of the way, with a nasty surprise climb just before the downhill home stretch. Along the way runners will pass many red sandstone rock formations and lush green meadows in summer. White Ranch is known for its various wildlife, including elk, deer, mountain lions, bobcats, bears, and wild turkeys. The view ranges from

Anissa Dorschner enjoys a partially white day on White Ranch.

great mesas to the east to snowcapped mountains to the west. Even Denver is visible between two mesas for much of the route.

White Ranch

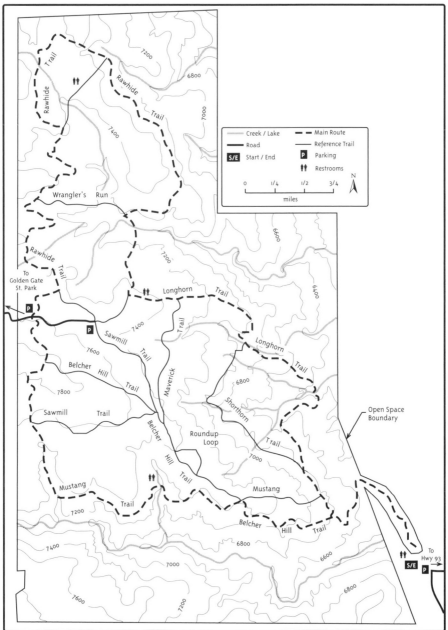

Rawhide Trail

7200

6800

Rawhide Trail

7000

7400

Creek / Lake

Road

S/E Start / End

Main Route

Reference Trail

P Parking

Restrooms

0   1/4   1/2   3/4   N

miles

Wrangler's   Run

6600

Rawhide Trail

7200

6400

To
Golden Gate
St. Park

P

P Sawmill

7400

Longhorn   Trail

Trail

Longhorn   Trail

7600

Belcher   Hill

Trail

Maverick

6800

Shorthorn

7800

Sawmill   Trail

Belcher

Roundup
Loop

Trail

Open Space
Boundary

7000

Hill

Mustang

Trail

Mustang

7200

Trail

Belcher   Hill   Trail

7400

6800

6600

To
Hwy 93

7000

S/E

P

7600

7200

6800

The "Norm"al Guy Says

"Hey, someone told me there might be a brewery around here somewhere. Can we finish this thing and go for the short beer tour?"

Trailhead Access

From Denver take I-70 west to Hwy. 58 west to Golden, then take Hwy. 93 north to Pine Ridge Road. Turn left and follow road to the parking lot.

Trail Description

From parking lot, take Belcher Hill Trail northwest. Stay left where Longhorn Trail intersects. At the top of the 2.2-mile climb, turn left onto Mustang Trail. Stay on this about 3 miles to the Rawhide Trail, and turn left again. Now heading north, follow Rawhide Trail around until it heads southeast, and 2 miles later turn left onto Longhorn Trail. Take this east and south all the way back to Belcher Hill Trail, about 3 miles, and make a left. Take Belcher the rest of the way back to the parking lot.

Alternative Route

For a shorter run, but no less hilly, follow directions to Mustang Trail. Take this west 1.8 miles up and turn right onto the Sawmill Trail. After about a mile of relatively flat terrain, turn right onto Belcher Hill Trail again, and return to your car.

Trail Notes

- Moderate to heavy bike traffic
- Light to moderate horse traffic
- Dogs must be on a leash at all times
- Outhouses in parking area and along the route
- No fee charged

Chapter 3

Boulder & Eldorado State Park

In Boulder, the flat farmlands of eastern Colorado crash into the foothills of the Rockies in a dramatic display of geology and ecology. A single trail run can take you from the sage and yucca of the prairie to the ponderosa pines and aspen of the mountains. Wildflower enthusiasts can enjoy blooms for months as spring travels from the lower elevations to the higher peaks.

Boulder's most recognized landmark is the Flatirons, a series of uplifted red sandstone formations that provide a beautiful backdrop to the city. Named for their resemblance to the bottom of old-fashioned irons, the Flatirons were formed 300 million years ago as the ancestral Rocky Mountains eroded and streams deposited layers of sand and pebbles that compacted into the Fountain Formation. When the modern Rocky Mountains uplifted 65 million years ago, the previously horizontal layers were thrust into nearly vertical positions.

In nearby Eldorado Canyon, you can view 1.7 billion years of geological history. The oldest igneous rock is found in the granite exposed at the west end of the park, while the slightly younger metamorphic quartzite is found in Supremacy Rock. Several slanted slabs of red sandstone belong to the same era as the Flatirons. But the Rotwand Wall is composed of Lyons Formation sandstone, formed a

One of Boulder's original trail runners, a mule deer, grazes in the transition zone between the flat plains of eastern Colorado and the Rocky Mountains.

mere 280 million years ago from sand blowing in from the great desert that once lay east of the mountains.

The rock formations of Boulder County have made it an international mecca of rock climbing, but they also provide spectacular scenery for trail runners.

In Boulder County you could run a different trail each day from May through September, thanks to 33,000 acres of public lands set aside for recreational use. Chautauqua Park, Eben G. Fine Park, and Mount Sanitas are favorite trailheads right in town. While running on local trails, we have seen bears, mountain lions, countless deer, coyotes, rattlesnakes, red foxes, golden and bald eagles, and other wildlife.

If there were a world capital of trail running, Boulder would be a likely candidate. On some of this college town's more popular trails, it is not uncommon to meet more runners than hikers. Top trail marathon runners Adam Chase and Lisa Goldsmith, and 1997 and 1998 Leadville Trail 100 champion Steve Peterson, call Boulder home. Local world-class road runners Arturo Barrios, Uta Pippig, and Gwyn Coogan often train on the trails to give their battered bodies a break. In writing this guidebook, the toughest task for us was to choose a small handful of our favorite trails that represent the range of options in our hometown.

Considering the number of trails and runners, it is ironic there are no official trail races in Boulder. For 10 years the clandestine Basic Boulder Mountain Marathon was (dis)organized by maverick runners Neal Beidleman and Kevin Cooney as an unofficial (translation: unpermitted) race among friends. The course changed each year to keep the runners and park rangers on their toes, and usually included ascents of several of Boulder's highest peaks, like Green and Bear Mountains, on the way to Eldorado Canyon and back.

Pressure from park managers who repeatedly denied permits for the race intensified as the field grew to more than one hundred runners. Facing pos-

sible arrest the race disorganizers finally quit. It was the tenth and final race that got Scott and Phil hooked on trail running. Rumor has it that small groups of nostalgic Basic Boulder veterans hit the trails each fall to memorialize the race.

Après-Run

It's a Boulder tradition to start weekend adventures with coffee, bagels, and diverse cream cheese spreads at Moe's Bagels, which has expanded from its original 2650 Broadway location to two additional shops, one on the Hill at 1116 13th and the other at 3075 Arapaho.

Our favorite postrun watering hole and restaurant is the Oasis Brewery at 4593 Broadway. Other great brew pubs include the Walnut Brewery at 1123 Walnut and the Mountain Sun Pub & Brewery at 1535 Pearl Street. The Hungry Toad at 2543 Broadway has delicious burgers, salads, and other fare, and Newcastle beer on tap.

Legal camping is virtually nonexistent in Boulder, but you can pitch a tent in several campgrounds near Nederland in the Roosevelt National Forest (303-444-6600) or at a private campground closer to town called the Boulder Mountain Lodge (303-444-0882).

Several bed and breakfast inns are located in some of the city's first homes, including the Boulder Victoria (303-938-1300), Inn on Mapleton Hill (303-449-6528), the Briar Rose (303-442-3007), and The Alps, 3 miles up scenic Boulder Canyon (303-938-1300). The elegant and historic Hotel

Boulderado is also a great place to stay and hear live music (303-444-5445).

Resources

Boulder Chamber of Commerce, 2440 Pearl Street, Boulder, CO 80302; 303-442-1044

Eldorado Canyon State Park, P.O. Box B, Eldorado Springs, CO 80025; 303-494-3943

City of Boulder Mountain Parks, Ranger Cottage, 9th and Baseline, Boulder, CO 80302; 303-441-3408

City of Boulder Open Space, 1300 Canyon Boulevard, Boulder, CO 80302; 303-441-3400

Roosevelt National Forest, 303-444-6600

Boulder Valley Ranch

—Scott Boulbol

Great for speed workouts, this loop is a classic plains trail run through yucca and prickly pear cactus over dirt road, gravel path, and single track with panoramic views of the Flatirons and Indian Peaks.

Time: 40–80 minutes
Distance: 5.75 miles
Start & End Elevation: 5,500 feet
Total Elevation Gain: 755 feet
High Point: 5,600 feet
Low Point: 5,200 feet
Best Season: Year-round
Support Points: None
Runability: 100%
Difficulty: Easy
Type: Loop
Map: "Trails in the Boulder Valley," City of Boulder Open Space and Mountain Parks, 1997
Contact: City of Boulder Open Space, 303-441-3400

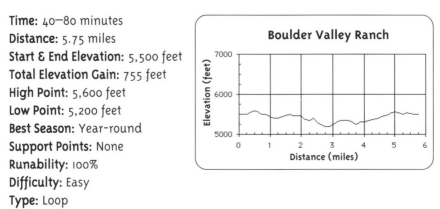

About the Trail

You don't have to climb 5,000 feet and freefall down a 40-degree single track to experience trail running's pleasures; there are plenty of exciting trails in the plains (though you may never find Phil on these trails). The Boulder Valley Ranch Open Space, just north of the city, is a vast expanse of mesas, gently rolling hills, and bucolic pastures. The miles of single-track trails and dirt roads are great for horses, bikes, and especially runners. World-class runners such as Arturo Barrios, Mark Coogan, Uta Pippig, and Gwyn Coogan like to do speed work on the relatively flat and well-maintained trails and dirt roads. The vistas of the mountains and foothills are unsurpassed. There are few trees, but native flora such as yucca and prickly pear cactus abound, along with a rainbow of wildflowers during early summer. Quite often, various birds of prey, including bald and golden eagles, can be seen circling overhead. The best way to experience all the intersecting trails is to explore—the chances of getting lost are slim. In winter the area is great for snowshoeing and cross-country skiing immediately after snowfall, but the snow melts quickly offering runners access year-round.

Trailhead Access

From downtown Boulder, head north on Broadway Avenue. At the edge of town where Broadway merges into Hwy. 36, take an immediate right onto a dirt road (North Broadway) and follow to the Foothills Trail parking area on the west side of the road.

Boulder Valley Ranch, a great place to run your dog and baby.

Trail Description

From the parking lot, run north 0.1 mile on North Broadway (dirt road), to the Degge trailhead on the east side of the road. Head east on the Degge Trail up and over the first ridge, to the Hidden Valley Trail, and turn right. Head south along the valley rim until the trail crosses the valley and continues up the opposite ridge. Run along the top of this mesa to the Mesa Reservoir Loop Trail, and turn right. Follow this trail east and then north to the Eagle Trail. A right turn here sends you east along another ridge, and then drops you down to a small pond. Continue up a short climb on the far side of the pond and turn left (west) onto the Sage Trail. Follow this trail past some stables

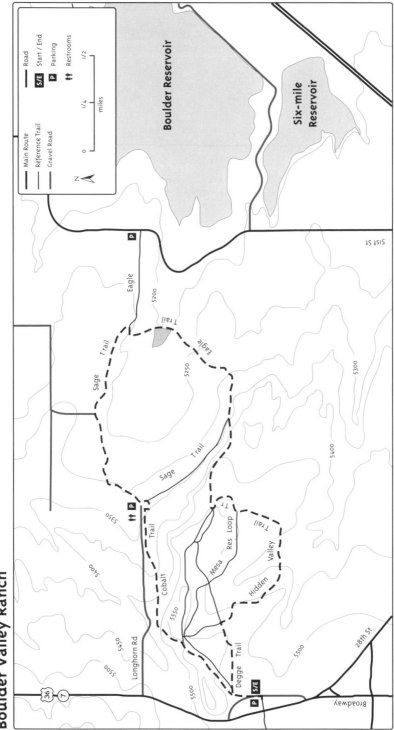

Boulder Valley Ranch

and up to the dirt road (Longhorn Road). Cross the road into the Boulder Valley Ranch parking area, go through the cattle gate, and turn right (west) onto the Cobalt Trail. This trail follows the road and then starts to veer left up the ridge. At the top of the ridge, follow the dirt road back to the parking area.

Alternative Route

By starting at the Wonderland Lake Open Space parking area, on Broadway Avenue in north Boulder, you can add about an hour to your run, while staying on relatively flat terrain. Take the Wonderland Lake Trail around the lake. On the west shore, head north up the hill on the Foothills Trail. Follow this trail north and continue across Lee Hill Road. At the top of the next climb, bear right to stay on Foothills Trail. Descend a rocky single track and continue through the tunnel under Hwy. 36 to the Foothills Trail parking area. From here, follow the above directions for the Boulder Valley Ranch Loop and return to the Wonderland Lake parking area the way you came.

Trail Notes
- Moderate foot traffic, high bike and horse traffic
- Outhouses at Boulder Valley Ranch parking area
- Bikes allowed on all trails except Mesa Reservoir Loop Trail, Degge Trail, and Hidden Valley Trail
- Dogs allowed: voice and sight control; leash must be used on Eagle Trail from February 1 to July 31; plenty of water for dog swimming and drinking
- No potable water
- No fee charged

Eldorado Canyon Trail

—Scott Boulbol

An out-and-back run following Eldorado Canyon over steep single track, with views of Eldorado's world-famous climbing routes, the Continental Divide, and Denver.

Time: 60–80 minutes
Distance: 5.5 miles
Start & End Elevation: 6,100 feet
Total Elevation Gain: 1,560 feet
High Point: 7,050 feet
Low Point: 6,100 feet
Best Season: Year-round
Support Points: None
Runability: 90–100%
Difficulty: Moderate
Type: Out-and-back
Map: "Trails in the Boulder Valley," City of Boulder Open Space and Mountain Parks, 1997
Contact: Eldorado Canyon State Park, 303-494-3943

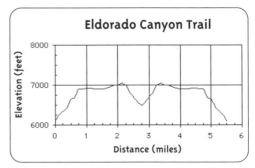

About the Trail

Just south of Boulder, Eldorado Canyon State Park is renowned for its towering sandstone and granite rock, upon which the best climbers in the world can be seen on any summer day. While climbers make their slow, laborious ascents up the rock walls, runners can quickly travel deep into the canyon and all the way up to south Boulder Creek on the Eldorado Canyon Trail. From many points along the route, a glance to the southeast reveals views of Denver, about 30 miles away, framed by the sheer canyon walls. To the west the foothills rise gradually to the Indian Peaks and the Great Divide. Precariously perched on the mountainside directly south of the canyon, coal trains make their way up over the mountain passes on their way to southwestern Colorado. Though it is only 10 minutes from downtown Boulder, this trail sees very little traffic and is surely one of the most peaceful runs in the area.

Trailhead Access

Take Broadway south out of Boulder. Head west on Eldorado Springs Drive (Hwy. 170), and continue through the small town of Eldorado Springs to the park entrance. After paying an inexpensive entrance fee, continue another mile to the west parking area. The trailhead is on the north side of the canyon near the parking area.

Eldorado Canyon Trail

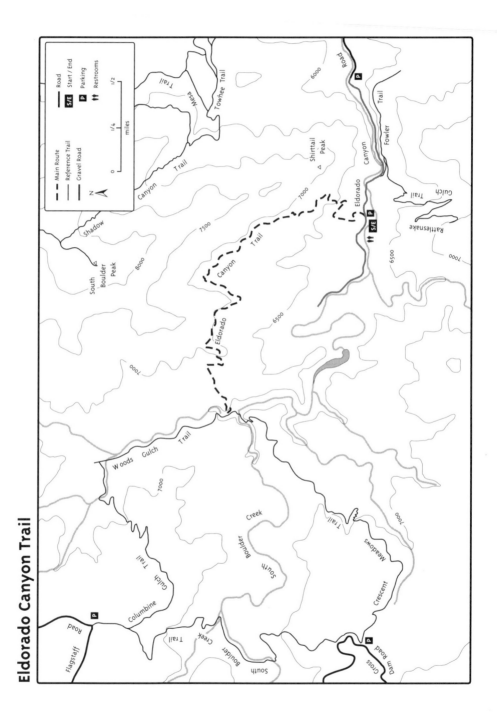

Scott and Taz Boulbol on a quest for gold doggy biscuits in Eldorado Canyon State Park.

Trail Description

With no intersections, this is an easy trail to follow. Head north up the trail from the west parking area, and follow the trail until it meets the Woods Gulch Trail. Turn back here and return to the parking lot.

Alternative Routes

You can add the Walker Ranch Loop to the Eldorado Canyon Trail to make a "lollipop loop." From the end of Eldorado Canyon Trail, turn right on the fire access road (Woods Gulch Trail). Climb the hill, then turn left onto Columbine Gulch Trail. Turn left on the South Boulder Creek Trail near the Walker Ranch parking area. Cross the creek at the bottom of the hill. After a steep climb, veer left onto the Crescent Meadows Trail. Follow this trail through the meadows, then down a steep hill to the creek. After crossing the creek, turn right back onto the Eldorado Canyon Trail. Adding the Walker Ranch Loop will make the total distance approximately 14 miles with a running time of 2 to 3 hours.

Another great way to add some mileage to the Eldorado Canyon Trail is to leave your car at the park entrance and enjoy the canyon by running the gravel road. The sandstone cliffs of Eldorado are truly amazing.

Trail Notes

- Light horse and foot traffic
- Dogs allowed: A leash, 6-foot or shorter, must be used at all times
- Bathrooms and water at trailhead
- State parks entry fee
- Bikes not allowed on the Eldorado Canyon Trail, but bike traffic is moderate to heavy on the Walker Ranch Loop

Green Mountain Loop
—Scott Boulbol

Cool and moist in the summer, this challenging single-track loop to the top of 8,144-foot Green Mountain covers smooth dirt trail, rugged single track, and steep rocky steps.

Time: 1.25–2.0 hours
Distance: 6 miles
Start & End Elevation: 5,620 feet
Total Elevation Gain: 2,854 feet
High Point: 8,144 feet
Low Point: 5,620 feet
Best Season: Year-round
Support Points: None
Runability: 90%
Difficulty: Moderate to difficult
Type: Lollipop loop
Map: "Trails in the Boulder Valley," City of Boulder Open Space and Mountain Parks, 1997
Contact: City of Boulder Mountain Parks, 303-441-3408

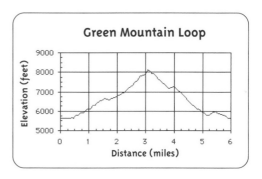

About the Trail
Green Mountain is so much more than a backdrop to Boulder's trademark red sandstone fins, the Flatirons. As testament to its challenge, the CU ski team and many pro ski racers use the 8,144-foot peak for dry land training. The route ascends the northern flank of Green Mountain where wildflowers, ferns, aspen, and pines grow in the moist shade. From the start at Chautauqua Park, to the west ridge, and especially at the summit, this trail offers spectacular views of the city to the east and the snowcapped Indian Peaks to the west. Green Mountain is a formidable foe as a first peak, but it is a goal well worth conquering.

Erica Greenwood races a late afternoon thunderstorm on the Greenman Trail.

Green Mountain Loop

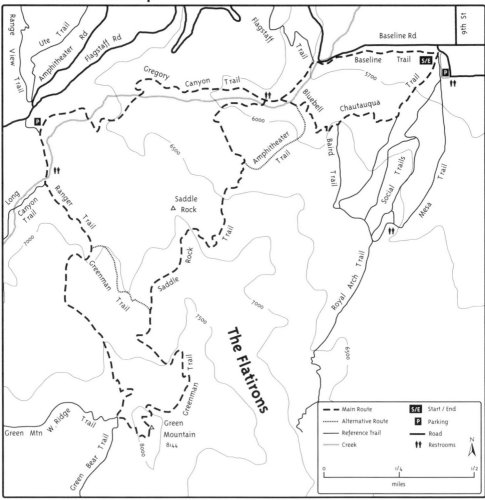

Trailhead Access

From Canyon and Broadway, head south on Broadway, then turn right on Baseline Road. After passing 9th Street, turn left into the Chautauqua parking area.

Trail Description

From the parking lot below the Chautauqua ranger station, head west on the Baseline Trail (an unmarked single track that runs parallel to Baseline Road). At the paved parking access road, veer left and continue to the Gregory Canyon parking lot. Follow the signs to the Gregory Canyon Trail. After about 1.2 miles of climbing, the trail levels off for a short jaunt through the pines, and then crosses a creek and veers south to the Gregory Canyon Lodge (more of a log pavilion than a lodge, but outhouses are provided). Turn left at the lodge onto the Ranger Trail and continue past the Greenman Trail intersection. Turn left at the intersection onto Green Mountain West Ridge Trail (east) and continue up the steep steps to the summit. After signing the summit log (make sure to include the ascent time, as it will surely impress the other summiters), head north down the Greenman Trail. Follow the Greenman Trail until you reach the Saddle Rock Trail, then turn right (east). Continue on Saddle Rock until you reach the Gregory Canyon parking area. Turn right (south) from the parking area and cross the stream on a small footbridge. Turn left onto a single track after the bridge, then take a quick right onto Bluebell Baird Trail. Turn left (east) onto the Chautauqua Trail and follow this trail back to the Chautauqua parking area.

Alternative Routes

On the return leg, staying on Greenman Trail until it connects with Ranger Trail provides a slightly longer run, but an easier downhill. Another variation is to come down the Amphitheater Trail, which is a right turn about two-thirds of the way down the Saddle Rock Trail. The Amphitheater

The "Norm"al Guy Says

"Oh no, not *ə$%#!! Green Mountain!"

Trail is an extremely challenging downhill due to steep stone and water bar steps and loose scree.

The alternative Green Mountain summit route of choice for pregnant women, lowlanders, and wimps is to drive up Flagstaff Road to the Green Mountain West Ridge trailhead. This trail is a direct easy route to the summit with just one short steep section near the top.

Trail Notes

- Light to moderate foot traffic
- Toilets and water at Chautauqua ranger station
- Outhouses at the lodge midway through the run
- Dogs allowed: voice and sight control; leash required at trailhead and in parking lots
- Bikes not allowed
- Winter ascents may require the use of crampons or studded running shoes
- No fee charged

Mount Sanitas Loop

—Phil Mislinski

Right in the middle of town, this vigorous loop covers steep single track with rocky steps to the top of 6,730-foot Mount Sanitas and a short, fast section of wide gravel path.

Time: 40–60 minutes
Distance: 3.3 miles
Start & End Elevation: 5,475 feet
Total Elevation Gain: 1,255 feet
High Point: 6,730 feet
Low Point: 5,475 feet
Best Season: Year-round
    (sometimes icy in winter)
Support Points: None
Runability: 90–100%
Difficulty: Moderate to difficult
Type: Loop
Map: "Trails in the Boulder Valley," City of Boulder Open Space and
    Mountain Parks, 1997
Contact: City of Boulder Open Space, 303-441-3400

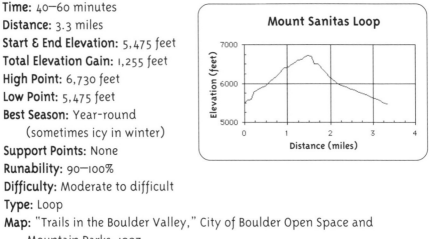

About the Trail

The Mount Sanitas Loop is one of the best hill climbs in Boulder, offering a quick and hearty summit, right near downtown. Gaining approximately 1,255 feet in under 1.5 miles, the Mount Sanitas Trail is a great place to build your quads and lungs. This short but difficult route has been described by one trail runner as "a great way to hork up your esophagus," but is completely runable if you can keep your lunch down on the climb up Mount Sanitas and are quick-footed on the East Ridge descent. It is actually faster and more pleasant to power hike the steeper sections of the climb up the West Ridge Trail. Considering the steepness of Mount Sanitas, we have decided to include the much easier Sanitas Valley/Dakota Ridge Loop as the alternative of choice.

Trailhead Access

From Broadway and Canyon in Boulder, head north on Broadway, turn left (west) on Mapleton Avenue. The Sanitas Valley trailhead and a small picnic shelter are on the north side of the street, just past the hospital.

Trail Description

From the picnic shelter, cross the small footbridge over the drainage creek.

Mount Sanitas Loop

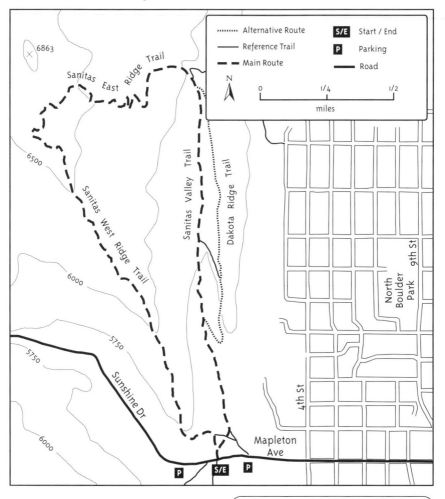

Veer left onto the Mount Sanitas West Ridge Trail and begin climbing almost immediately. Continue up until you reach the metal post at the summit, get discouraged, "hork up your esophagus," or die. Once reaching the top, don't forget to enjoy the views of Boulder to the east and the Indian Peaks to the west that you just worked so hard to see. From the metal post, head down the steep and technical East Ridge Trail

The "Norm"al Guy Says

"You guys are absolutely sick. If I wanted to kill myself, I would just use a gun and get it over with quickly. I'll stick to the Dakota Ridge Loop and meet you for beers afterward."

that runs into the top of the smooth Sanitas Valley Trail. Continue down the Sanitas Valley Trail to the parking

Rob Chesher used hard training on Mount Sanitas and great aerodynamics to achieve eighth place at the 1997 Pikes Peak Marathon.

area or immediately veer left onto the more rugged Dakota Ridge Trail, which rejoins the Sanitas Valley Trail near the bottom.

Alternative Route

If you want to do a quick, 2.4-mile, 20–30 minute, casual loop with only 525 feet of elevation gain, use the following directions: From the picnic shelter, head north then veer right onto the Sanitas Valley Trail. After 0.15 mile, turn right onto the Dakota Ridge Trail at the signpost. Continue along Dakota Ridge until you reach the top of Sanitas Valley. Return by coming down the Sanitas Valley Trail.

Trail Notes

• Light to moderate foot traffic
• Limited parking in the lots; street parking available to the east
• High dog-walking traffic on Sanitas Valley Trail
• Dogs allowed: voice and sight control at all times; leash required at trailhead and in parking lots
• Bikes not allowed
• No fee charged

South Mesa Trail Loop

—Phil Mislinski

A scenic loop over rocky single-track and gravel path with gentle climbs/descents and views of famous rock climbs.

Time: 40–60 minutes
Distance: 4.8 miles
Start & End Elevation: 5,550 feet
Total Elevation Gain: 1,110 feet
High Point: 6,610 feet
Low Point: 5,550 feet
Best Season: Year-round
Support Points: None
Runability: 100%
Difficulty: Easy to moderate
Type: Loop
Map: "Trails in the Boulder Valley," City of Boulder Open Space and Mountain Parks, 1997
Contact: City of Boulder Mountain Parks, 303-441-3408

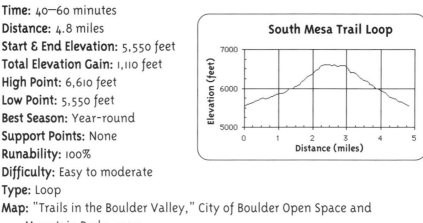

About the Trail

This loop is a great after- or before-work run, taking approximately 45 minutes to complete. Along the way you get incredible views of legendary rock climbing formations such as Devil's Thumb, the Maiden, Jamcrack Spire, Tower of the Moon, and the Matron. You will also encounter a wide variety of terrain, including technical rocky single track, smooth gravel fire access road, and easy climbs and descents.

Trailhead Access

From Broadway Avenue and Table Mesa Road in Boulder, head south on Broadway, which turns into State Hwy. 93. After 2.4 miles, turn right toward Eldorado Springs State Park on Hwy.

Early morning scenery along the Big Bluestem Trail.

South Mesa Trail Loop

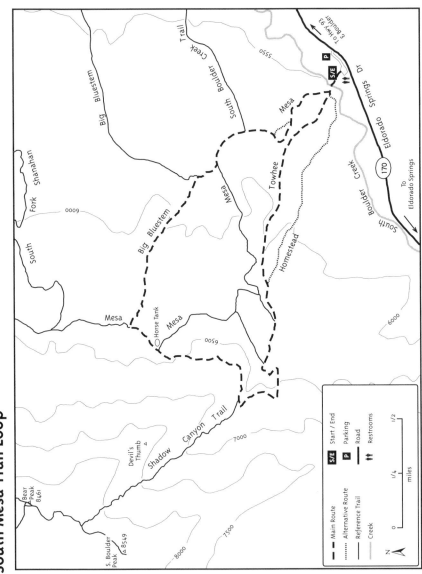

The "Norm"al Guy Says

"Great loop. It is short enough to avoid dehydration, exhaustion, starvation, and death. The moderate climbs make it easy to keep the cookies down."

170. You will see the Mesa trailhead parking area on the right after 1.6 miles.

Trail Description

Head north from the parking lot and cross South Boulder Creek on the footbridge. Veer right onto Mesa Trail. Follow the smooth trail for about 3 minutes, then turn right (north) onto an unmarked rocky single track. Turn right (north) when the single track rejoins the smooth trail after about 0.25 mile. Pass the South Boulder Creek Trail signpost, then turn right at the next signpost onto Big Bluestem Trail. After 0.25 mile, take the left fork of Big Bluestem and head west. (If for some reason you take the right fork, you will end up in a cow pasture that really is not all that exciting.) Continue west on Big Bluestem until you reach Mesa Trail. Turn left (south) and follow Mesa Trail until you reach a horse watering tank, then veer right onto the Shadow Canyon cutoff trail. Stay on the gently rolling single track until you reach the mouth of Shadow Canyon. Cross the small stream and head south on the fire access road. Follow the steep, smooth, winding downhill until you reach the Towhee Trail intersection, then veer right on Towhee Trail. The Towhee Trail ends at the footbridge over South Boulder Creek near the parking area.

Alternative Route

Once on Towhee Trail, veer right onto Homestead Trail to get a good view of the South Boulder Creek Valley. This route ends at the same place and is about the same distance.

Trail Notes
• Light to moderate foot traffic
• Horse traffic moderate to heavy on weekends
• Outhouses at trailhead
• Dogs allowed: voice and sight control at all times; leash required at trailhead and parking area
• Bikes not allowed
• No potable water
• No fee charged

Chapter 4

Fort Collins

Located just east of the mountains of northern Colorado, Fort Collins has a rich agricultural past. Fur traders and trappers camped under the majestic cottonwood trees lining the Cache la Poudre River west of town as far back as the 1840s. But the first residents of Fort Collins were frustrated gold prospectors who built farms and ranches instead. An agricultural colony was established in the 1870s, and to keep the riffraff away, lots were only sold to nondrinking, upstanding citizens.

Ironically, the town is now a showcase of Colorado microbreweries. The Colorado State University, founded in 1879 as the Agricultural College of Colorado, has grown from 5,000 to 20,000 students. And while farming and ranching remain important to both the university and the town, the high-tech industry is also booming there.

Like other Front Range communities, Fort Collins is spreading fast with new neighborhoods springing up in the suburbs virtually overnight. In the epicenter is Old Town, the original downtown with its brick and false-fronted buildings restored in the 1980s. A pedestrian mall encourages visitors and residents alike to enjoy the many art galleries, brew pubs, and shops located in Old Town.

Bodies of water abound in the Fort Collins area. Small lakes, ponds, and larger reservoirs supply water for agri-

Phil Mislinski enjoys a sunny afternoon on the Greyrock Trail. Photo by Monique Cole.

cultural, residential, and recreational purposes. The most popular of them all, Horsetooth Reservoir, holds almost 4,000 acres of water, which fishermen, boaters, and water-skiers enjoy. Surrounded by beautiful bluffs and with its many inlets and coves, Horsetooth looks like a miniature version of Utah's Lake Powell.

The Cache la Poudre River feeds all these bodies of water as it flows east from the Rocky Mountains. French for "hide the powder," the river was named by French fur trappers who cached large barrels of gunpowder along its banks to avoid carrying them long distances. Following the river west from Fort Collins along Hwy. 14, drivers are greeted by the stunning granite cliffs of Poudre Canyon. Rock climbers hover above as rafters and kayakers run the rapids of the Poudre below.

Après-Run

The gem of Old Town's microbreweries is Coopersmith's Pub and Brewing Company at #5 Old Town Square. Head there for delicious, varied lunch and dinners and a choice of five beers (and three sodas) brewed on the premises. If you're in Poudre Canyon, head up Hwy. 14 (15 miles west of Hwy. 287) to the Mishawaka Inn. The view from the riverside patio is unsurpassed, and nationally known bands play live there on summer Saturday nights.

You can also enjoy a view of the Poudre from a tent campsite within Roosevelt National Forest. Reservations for Mountain Park, Dowdy, West Lake, and Chambers Campgrounds can be made by calling 1-800-280-CAMP. Even more campgrounds are found farther up the canyon. Several hundred campsites ring Carter, Flatiron, Pinewood, and Horsetooth Reservoirs. Call

the Larimer County Parks for more information, 970-226-4517.

Most of the national hotel and motel chains provide lodging in Fort Collins, many near the junction of I-25 and Hwy. 287. A number of quaint bed and breakfast inns and lodges are located in Old Town and up the Poudre Canyon. Contact the Convention and Visitor's Bureau for more information (see Resources).

Resources

Fort Collins Convention and Visitor's Bureau, 420 S. Howes Street, Suite 101; P.O. Box 1998, Fort Collins, CO 80522; 970-482-5821 or 800-274-3678

Roosevelt National Forest, Redfeather/Estes-Poudre Ranger District Offices, 1311 S. College Avenue, Fort Collins, CO 80524; 970-498-2770

Horsetooth Mountain and Reservoir Parks, Larimer County Parks Department, 1800 S. County Road 31, Loveland, CO 80537; 970-226-4517

Lory State Park, 708 Lodgepole Drive, Bellevue, CO 80512; 970-493-1623

Arthur's Rock Loop

—Scott Boulbol

A steep up-and-down loop of single-track trail in the foothills above Horsetooth Reservoir in Lory State Park. The summit is a stunning rock formation called Arthur's Rock.

Time: 1.0–1.5 hours
Distance: 4.8 miles
Start & End Elevation: 5,480 feet
Total Elevation Gain: 1,520 feet
High Point: 6,840 feet
Low Point: 5,480 feet
Best Season: Year-round
Support Points: None
Runability: 90–100%
Difficulty: Moderate
Type: Loop
Map: USGS Horsetooth Reservoir Quadrangle, Lory State Park Info. Map
Contact: Lory State Park, 970-493-1623

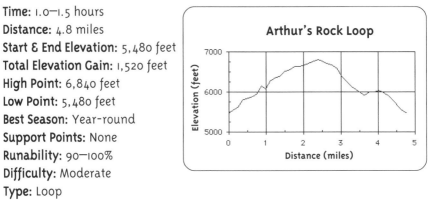

Phil Mislinski enjoys one of the few flat sections of the Arthur's Rock Loop. Photo by Scott Boulbol.

About the Trail

Just west of Fort Collins are two of the great mountain trail running areas on the Front Range. Lory State Park and Horsetooth Reservoir offer many miles of single-track trails and dirt roads with wonderful views of the mountains to the west and Horsetooth Reservoir to the east. These are relatively un-crowded, and often quite challenging, mountainous trails. One of our favorite loops in the area is the Arthur's Rock Loop in Lory State Park. This is a formidable loop, but one that can be done after work or on a lunch hour. It begins with a very steep climb up a canyon for about 2 miles. Then a flat section at the top leads to the rewarding view of the rock formation. Take a

Arthur's Rock Loop

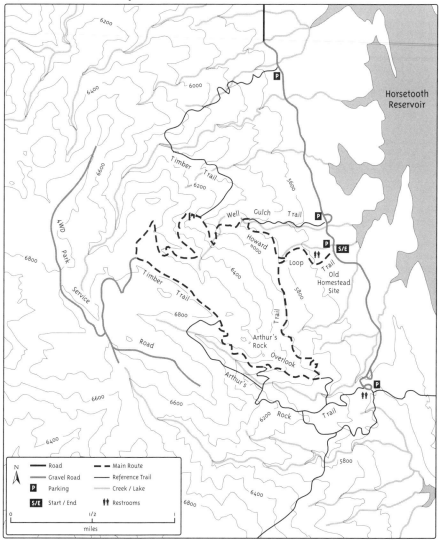

breather here to enjoy the spectacular panorama, then prepare for a screaming downhill almost all the way home. This comes as a welcome relief from the grinding climb, even if I do have to watch Phil blast by me soon after we begin the descent (and I thought I had buried him on the way up).

Trailhead Access

Heading north on Hwy. 287 from Fort Collins, signs will indicate the way to Lory State Park, which is easier than following the alphabet soup of roads with letters in their names that don't correspond with compass points. From Hwy. 287, turn left onto 54E Road and look for 25E Road. Turn left here, veering left to stay on 25E Road, then make a right onto 23 Road. Veer right onto 25G Road, which leads into Lory State Park. Once inside the park, look for the Old Homestead Site parking area on the right. The trail is just west of this parking area.

Trail Description

From the parking area, take the Howard Loop Trail west about 0.5 mile to the intersection with the Overlook Trail. Stay on Howard Loop Trail, which veers to the right, and continue climbing west to the intersection with the Timber Trail. A left here and a little more climbing will bring you to a campsite and a four-wheel-drive service road. Stay on the Timber Trail another mile to Arthur's Rock. From the rock there are two ways down, but take the one nearest the rock formation, and this will descend to the Overlook Trail. Turn left again to stay on the Overlook Trail back to the Howard Loop Trail. Turn right here and drop down to the parking area.

The "Norm"al Guy Says

"If I keep staring at Horsetooth Reservoir on this downhill, I may end up with *no* teeth."

Alternative Route

There is also a great one-way trail in the park, if you have two cars. Drop one at the parking area at the entrance to the park, and drive the other to the parking area at the end of the park. Take the Arthur's Rock Trail south from the parking lot. This quickly loops back to the west and climbs up to the rock formation. From here take the Timber Trail north, and remain on this until it drops back down to the first car at the entrance to the park.

Trail Notes

• Moderate foot traffic
• Dogs allowed on a leash
• Bathrooms at start
• Bikes are not allowed on most of this loop (they are allowed on several trails in the park)
• State park entry fee

Greyrock Loop

—Phil Mislinski

A mostly rocky and technical single track that takes you high above Poudre Canyon on the way to the summit of Greyrock and back. The smooth gradual sections of trail make the climbs more than worth the effort.

Time: 1.5–2.0 hours
Distance: 7 miles
Start & End Elevation: 5,580 feet
Total Elevation Gain: 2,580 feet
High Point: 7,600 feet
Low Point: 5,580 feet
Best Season: Spring through fall
Support Points: None
Runability: 90–100%
Difficulty: Moderate
Type: Loop
Map: Trails Illustrated Number 101
Contact: Roosevelt National Forest, 970-498-2770

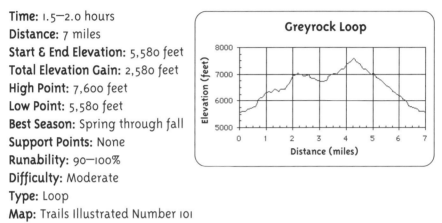

About the Trail

This is one of those loops that can only be described as amazing. For the most part the trail is steep, rocky, and very technical. However, each technical section is relatively short and the rewards are well worth the effort. Every time the trail seems to be getting too steep or difficult you suddenly find yourself on a gentle grade, smooth switchback, or at the top of a climb. You always end up with a great view to distract you or a casual section of trail when you really need it. The meadow below Greyrock is so beautiful that we turned around and ran it again so we could see it in both directions. We would have done it a few more times if it weren't for an afternoon thunderstorm.

Samantha Cole Mislinski works on her downhill running technique on the Greyrock Trail.

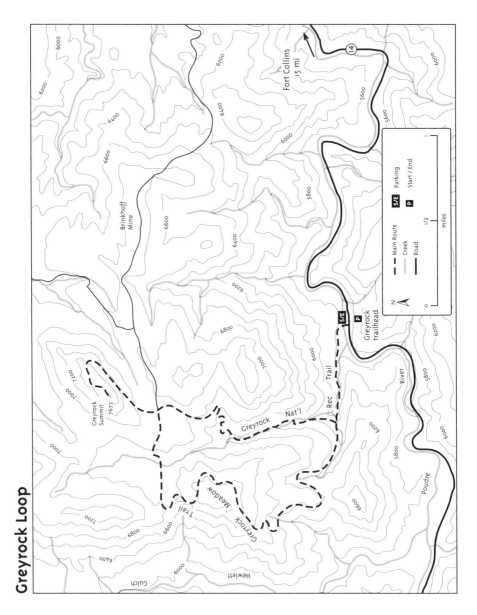

Greyrock Loop

Trailhead Access

From Fort Collins take Hwy. 287 north to Hwy. 14, then head west on Hwy. 14. Continue up Poudre Canyon 8.2 miles to the Greyrock parking area on the left.

The "Norm"al Guy Says

"Every time I was about to die on a climb, it was suddenly over, and I managed to hang on for more abuse."

Trail Description

From the parking lot, go down the concrete steps and cross Hwy. 14 to the trailhead. Cross the river on the bridge and veer left onto the Greyrock National Recreation Trail. At the intersection continue straight onto the Greyrock Meadow Trail and begin the climb to the high ridge. Follow the trail as it winds north through a large open meadow below Greyrock. Continue up a short climb on the far side of the meadow. Enter another smaller meadow where you reach the intersection with the Greyrock Summit Trail and the Greyrock National Recreation Trail. Turn left to do the quick out-and-back to Greyrock Summit (0.5 mile each way). When you get back to the intersection, turn left to go down the Greyrock National Recreation Trail and complete the loop. When you reach the lower intersection with the Greyrock Meadow Trail, turn left to get back to the parking lot.

Alternative Route

If you prefer your steeper sections of trail to be uphills, do the loop in the opposite direction from what is described above.

Trail Notes

- Bikes are not allowed
- Horses are not allowed
- No potable water or toilets
- Moderate foot traffic
- Dogs must be on a leash at all times
- No fee charged

Horsetooth Falls Loop

—Phil Mislinski

A scenic loop over varying terrain with moderate to difficult climbs/descents and views of Horsetooth Reservoir and Horsetooth Rock.

Time: 1.25–2.5 hours
Distance: 8.4 miles
Start & End Elevation: 5,762 feet
Total Elevation Gain: 2,188 feet
High Point: 5,600 feet
Low Point: 5,200 feet
Best Season: Year-round
Support Points: None
Runability: 90–100%
Difficulty: Moderate
Type: Loop
Map: Horsetooth Reservoir Quadrangle, USGS and Horsetooth Mountain Park trail map (available at trailhead)
Contact: Larimer County Parks Department, 970-226-4517

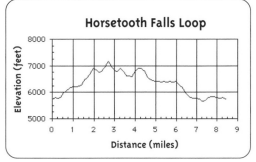

Horsetooth Falls Loop

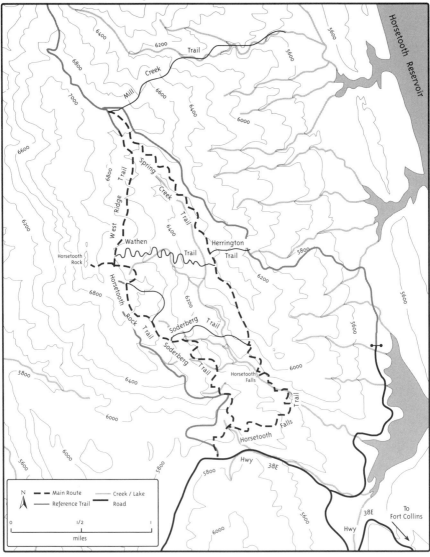

About the Trail

This is one of the best moderate loops in the Horsetooth Reservoir area. Circling most of the Horsetooth Mountain Park, this run takes you through open meadows and pine groves to the base of Horsetooth Rock then down around to Horsetooth Falls. The terrain ranges from smooth to rocky single track with technical difficulty from easy to treacherous. All of the steep climbs are relatively short and runable. You are rewarded at the top of each

A very steep but well-maintained climb on the Horsetooth Falls Loop.

climb with incredible views of Horsetooth Reservoir and the surrounding bluffs. Even though the user traffic is fairly high in this park, it is relatively spread out. You will go for a few miles without seeing another person on the upper portions of this loop.

Trailhead Access

From I-25 take exit 265 and head west on Harmony Road. Turn right (north) on Taft Hill Road. After 0.5 mile turn left (west) on Hwy. 38E and follow it around the southern tip of the reservoir until you reach the Horsetooth Mountain Park lot on the right.

Trail Description

Leave the parking area on the trail marked for hikers. Veer left at the first fork to stay on the Soderberg Trail.

Turn left at the next intersection toward Horsetooth Rock. After 0.25 mile take the left fork, which is marked for hikers (the right fork is marked for horses and bikes). Continue until you reach the intersection with the Wathen Trail 0.25 mile below Horsetooth Rock. If you are interested in adding 0.5 mile to your run, do the quick up-and-back to the base of Horsetooth Rock (the views are well worth the effort). Head north on the Wathen Trail and veer left on the West Ridge Trail after approximately 0.1 mile (keep your eyes open because this turn is easy to miss). Follow the West Ridge Trail 1.5 miles until you reach a dirt service road. Continue north on the service road approximately 0.25 mile until you reach the intersection with the Spring Creek Trail and the Mill Creek Trail (the sign for these trails faces the other direction so be sure to pay attention). Continue down the Spring Creek Trail past the intersections with the Herrington Trail and Wathen Trail until you reach the top of Horsetooth Falls. Go around the falls on the obvious trail to the north of the falls and follow this around to the bottom edge of the falls where the trail intersects the Horsetooth Falls Trail. Turn right to do the quick out-and-back to the bottom of the falls or turn left if you don't think you can handle the extra 0.1 mile. Follow the Horsetooth Falls Trail 1 mile south, then west back to the second intersection with the Soderberg Trail. Veer left to follow the Soderberg Trail back to the parking area.

Alternative Route

Remain on Wathen Trail rather than veering left onto the West Ridge Trail. Descending Wathen Trail will shorten the loop by 1.75 miles, but you will encounter slightly rougher terrain.

Trail Notes

- Bikes are allowed (traffic can be heavy on the weekends)
- Horse traffic moderate to heavy on weekends
- Light to moderate foot traffic (fairly heavy near the trailhead)
- Outhouses at trailhead
- No potable water
- Dogs must be on a leash at all times; loose dogs may be impounded
- Daily parking fee at trailhead (annual passes are also available)

Chapter 5

Colorado Springs

Pikes Peak looms over Colorado Springs, a lone majestic 14,110-foot mountain that dwarfs its neighboring foothills. During the gold rush of 1859, eager miners heading for south-central Colorado painted "Pikes Peak or Bust" on their wagons. From its lofty heights, Katharine Lee Bates was inspired to write the anthem, *America the Beautiful.*

In November 1806, when Lt. Zebulon Pike failed to reach the summit of his namesake peak, he declared, "I believe no human being could have ascended to its pinnacle." Each August 1,800 runners prove that Zebulon was a mama's boy by funneling onto the narrow Barr Trail and running to its pinnacle in the Pikes Peak Ascent 13-mile run. The following day another 800 runners do the "round-trip" in the country's fourth oldest marathon. The Pikes Peak Marathon record time of 3 hours, 16 minutes, 39 seconds was set in 1993 by Matt "The Lung" Carpenter. But other runners, as well as Zebulon Pike, might assert that Carpenter is no human being. If you are interested in doing either of these races, get your entry form in early. They usually fill to capacity months before the race.

Many trail runners live in the shadow of Pikes Peak, including Carpenter, the world's best high-altitude marathoner. And most of the trails in the Colorado Springs area either have

Colorado Springs local Ed Boggess not only provided great trail information, he also provided a great photo opportunity during the Pikes Peak Marathon.

views of "The Peak" as locals call Pikes, or they wind along its flanks.

About 60 million years ago, the peak began to rise as a great dome from the flat alluvial fans deposited by ancient rivers. As it rose, it tore up the layers of sedimentary rock, tilting them up vertically. Wind and rain wore away at the softer rock, leaving behind the harder rock in the otherworldly shapes like the fins, towers, and spires found in Garden of the Gods National Landmark. These natural wonders attract almost six million tourists per year to the Colorado Springs area.

Each summer, hordes of camera toters flock to Pikes Peak and Garden of the Gods as well as the series of cascades at Seven Falls, the stalactites and stalag-mites of Cave of the Winds, and the sce-nic North and South Cheyenne Canyons. Then there are the man-made attractions, bordering on cheesy. In 1907 Anasazi cliff dwellings were disassembled and transported 350 miles to their new home at the Manitou Cliff Dwellings. The North Pole and Santa's Workshop cel-ebrates the consumerism of Christmas all year long at the base of Pikes Peak.

And even the natural wonders have been "improved." A laser light show brings a carnival atmosphere to Cave of the Winds, and the entire South Cheyenne Canyon and Seven Falls are illuminated with over a thousand col-orful lights. An elevator carved into the rock hoists visitors 130 feet to a view-point of Seven Falls, and both a cog railway and a well-maintained road lead to the summit of Pikes Peak that re-sembles a truck stop complete with park-ing lot and snack shop. Thankfully, there are still ample opportunities to earn your views on unspoiled trails.

Nestled at the foot of the Rampart Range, the U.S. Air Force Academy is also a popular tourist attraction. Most of the 18,500-acre campus is rolling, wooded hills and the campus is also a game refuge where deer and wild tur-keys abound. While most visitors flock to the planetarium and the seventeen-spire Cadet Chapel, we found the trails the best way to tour the campus.

The climate of Colorado Springs is mild, even by Front Range standards. Protected from storms by two natural barriers—the Rocky Mountains to the west and the Monument Divide to the north—the city receives an average of only 37 inches of snow annually. Winter average high temperatures range from 41° to 49°F, and summer highs are in the low to mid-80s, providing comfort-able running weather almost year-round.

Après-Run

For a healthy breakfast, lunch, or din-ner, head to Adam's Mountain Cafe (110 Canon Avenue) in Manitou Springs for natural food served in a pleasant setting with hanging plants and soft music. For a lively dinner or yard of ale, check out the Golden Bee, a real historic British pub reassembled across from the Broadmoor that has live sing-along ragtime piano music.

Since it is such a popular destina-tion, Colorado Springs has a great va-riety and number of accommodations from campgrounds to first-rate hotels (call the Convention & Visitor's Bureau at 800-DO-VISIT). But it only has one hotel that has joined a small handful of hotels nationally to be awarded Mobil's five-star rating. Located at the base of Cheyenne Mountain, the el-egant Broadmoor resort with its an-tique interiors, stately grounds, and world-class spa is a great place to luxu-riate after a long day of getting sweaty on the trails. A destination in itself, it's worth a visit even if you can't af-ford the room rates. Call 800-634-7711 for information and reservations.

A number of campgrounds are lo-cated in the Pike National Forest near Woodland Park and Rampart Reser-voir. The majority can be reserved (at least 10 days in advance) by calling 1-800-280-CAMP. As the campgrounds fill up early in the summer, reservations are a good idea. For additional camping information call the Pikes Peak Ranger District Office at 719-636-1602.

Resources

Pike National Forest, Pikes Peak Ranger District Office, 601 S. Weber Street, Colorado Springs, CO 80829; 719-636-1602

Colorado Springs Convention & Visitor's Bureau, 104 S. Cascade Avenue, Colorado Springs, CO 80829; 800-DO-VISIT or 719-635-1632

Colorado Springs Chamber of Commerce, P.O. Drawer B, Colorado Springs, CO 80829; 719-635-1551

Manitou Springs Chamber of Commerce, 354 Manitou Avenue, Manitou Springs, CO 80929; 719-685-5089

U.S. Air Force Academy Visitor's Center, HQ USAFA/PAV, 2346 Academy Drive, USAFA, CO 80840-9400; 719-333-4040

Barr Trail

—Scott Boulbol & Phil Mislinski

A classic trail run up and down the world-famous Pikes Peak. Mostly single track, with a small amount of dirt fire road, this trail climbs and descends almost 7,500 feet each with a high point of 14,110 feet.

Time: 4.0–7.0 hours
Distance: 22.5 miles
Start & End Elevation: 6,780 feet
Total Elevation Gain: 7,490 feet
High Point: 14,110 feet
Low Point: 6,780 feet
Best Season: Midsummer to early fall
Support Points: Summit House and Barr Camp
Runability: 70–90%
Difficulty: Extremely difficult
Type: Out-and-back
Map: Trails Illustrated Number 137
Contact: Pike National Forest Rangers, 719-636-1602

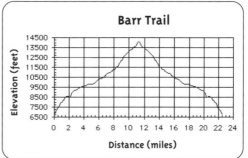

About the Trail

Each year the Barr Trail hosts the Pikes Peak Marathon, the fourth oldest marathon in the country—incredible considering its intense climbing and extremely high altitude. In August 1999 the Pikes Peak Marathon will celebrate

Barr Trail

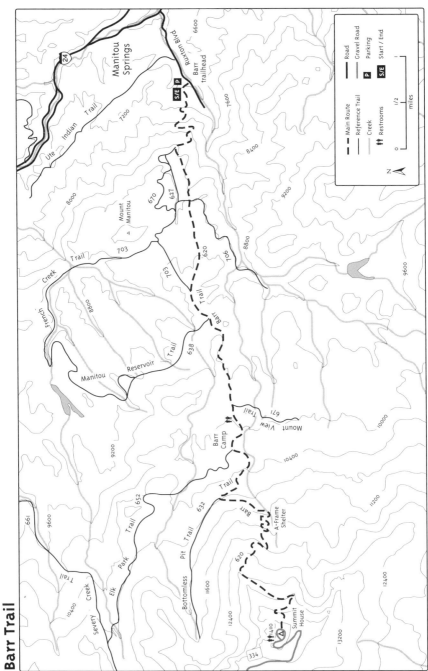

its forty-fourth birthday. This is not only an extremely challenging trail, but also one of the most rewarding and spectacular. The trail is amazingly smooth most of the way up, including the miles above treeline and through the talus near the top, making it almost completely runable. Of course, if you are local "human lung" Matt Carpenter, it is all easily runable in just over 3 hours round-trip! With almost 7,500 feet of climb, this run should not be taken lightly. And because of its length and height, beware of lightning and hypothermia. Do not attempt this trail unless you are in great shape with hours of training above 11,000 feet. Every year there are scores of runners who turn green during the marathon and puke their guts out along the side of the trail. Several are hauled off the mountain by race volunteers and paramedics. Once ready, run this for the experience of the terrain and scenery, and—unless you are doing the race— forget about the time. This one is too special to worry about pace and finishing time—simply enjoy.

Trailhead Access

From Colorado Springs head west on Hwy. 24 and exit in Manitou Springs. From the main street in Manitou, follow signs south to the Cog Railway. Just past the depot, turn right on Hydro Street. At the top of the short, steep

Neal Beidleman smiles at the thought of a cold beer waiting for him at the end of the Pikes Peak Marathon.

road, you will find the trailhead and parking for the Barr Trail.

Trail Description

Barr Trail is very easy to follow along its entire length. There are a handful of well-marked junctions with other trails; just take the one marked Barr Trail or To Pikes Peak Summit. When in doubt, head up. After reaching the summit house, descend the way you came. By entering either the Pikes Peak Marathon or the Ascent (with free bus rides down the mountain), you will get aid stations along the way and lots of camaraderie.

Alternative Routes

To shorten this route, but retain the high-altitude section, drive to the top of Pikes Peak via the Pikes Peak Toll Road. Start at the summit and run down the Barr Trail until ready to turn around and climb back to the summit. We suggest making it down to the Barr Camp, for a round-trip of about 3 hours. This can also be done as a one-way trip, from Manitou Springs to the summit. Just arrange for a ride to meet you at the top.

Trail Notes

• Very heavy foot traffic July–September; moderate to heavy during spring and fall
• Dogs allowed on a leash
• Bathrooms at summit; food and water available at summit
• Potable water and pit toilets at Barr Camp
• Light bike traffic
• Shelters at Barr Camp, the A-frame, and summit
• No fee charged

Falcon Trail

—*Phil Mislinski*

A 12-mile loop of rolling single-track and jeep roads with views of the foothills and Pikes Peak.

Time: 2.0–3.0 hours
Distance: 12 miles
Start & End Elevation: 6,920 feet
Total Elevation Gain: 1,010 feet
High Point: 7,360 feet
Low Point: 6,700 feet
Best Season: Year-round (best in late spring)
Support Points: Any of the many road crossings
Runability: 100%
Difficulty: Moderate
Type: Loop
Map: Trails Illustrated Number 137
Contact: U.S. Air Force Academy Visitor's Center, 719-333-4040

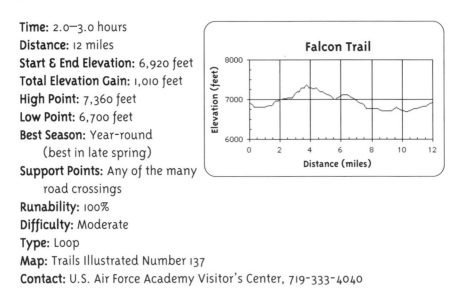

About the Trail

If you ever wanted to tour the Air Force Academy grounds, this is the best way to go. The mostly single-track trail winds through dense pine groves, over several creeks, and through meadows filled with wildflowers as it makes its way around the Academy. Most of the climbs are moderate to gentle; however, there are a few short and steep sections of technical single track. The trail is open to all hikers, horseback riders, and mountain bikers, but the Air Force recom-

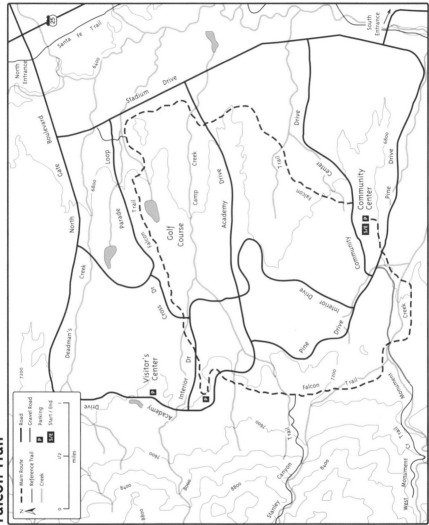

mends that you stay on the trail. This is especially important when cadet training activities are taking place.

Trailhead Access

From Colorado Springs, head north on I-25 and take the Air Force Academy South Entrance exit. Head west on South Gate Boulevard, then turn right on Stadium Drive. Take a left onto Community Center Drive, then a left into the Community Center parking lot. The trailhead is on the south side of the parking lot (immediately south of Building 5132, Youth Center), and it is marked with a large blue sign.

Air Force Academy graduate, "General" Rob Rysavy, plays tour guide on the Falcon Trail.

Trail Description

This trail is maintained by Boy Scout Troop 78 and for the most part they do a *great* job of marking the trail with blue signs that have a white, yellow, or red falcon emblem. From the parking lot, head down the steep and loose single track to the first road crossing. As with all the road crossings, keep your eyes open so you can easily spot where the trail picks up on the other side. (Due to construction and secondary trails, this is not always a trivial task for first-time Falcon loopers—look for the signs.) Begin heading west, then north while crossing Monument Creek

> ### The "Norm"al Guy Says
> "I can't believe that I was able to run a trail for 12 miles without having to walk. The best part was that it was actually fun!"

and Stanley Canyon Creek multiple times. Continue north past the Stanley Canyon Trail until you cross Academy Drive (if you find yourself heading continually west up a steep single track, you went the wrong way). Next, cross Interior Drive then Cross Drive about 0.33 mile later. Climb up onto the ridge above the golf course and pass a small reservoir on your right. Drop down to the south and enter a grove of pine trees. Follow the single track to the south as it parallels Stadium Drive, then cross Camp Creek and Academy Drive for the final push back to the Community Center.

Alternative Route

Do the loop in the opposite direction.

Trail Notes

- Light horse, mountain bike, and foot traffic
- Dogs allowed: Your dog must be on a leash at all times
- Water available at the Community Center Complex and Visitor's Center

Jones Park Trail
—*Phil Mislinski*

An out-and-back run that takes you to the source of Bear Creek and beyond over moderate to steep single track.

Time: 2.0–3.5 hours
Distance: 11.2 miles
Start & End Elevation: 7,840 feet
Total Elevation Gain: 2,500 feet
High Point: 10,120 feet
Low Point: 7,840 feet
Best Season: Year-round
Support Points: None
Runability: 90–100%
Difficulty: Moderate
Type: Out-and-back
Map: Trails Illustrated Number 137
Contact: Pike National Forest, 719-636-1602

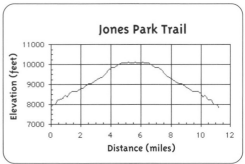

About the Trail

Starting from High Drive just north of the North Cheyenne Canyon Park, this run provides incredible views of Pikes Peak, the Garden of the Gods, Colorado Springs, the Broadmoor resort, and a handful of waterfalls. After getting the views from the ridge between Mount Buckhorn and Kineo Mountain, the trail drops down to Bear Creek where it passes through dense conifers and aspen groves as it follows the creek to its source. The trail ends at 10,000 feet when it intersects with a spur off the Seven Lakes Road (four-wheel-drive road). Even though the Jones Park Trail is a multiuse trail (hikers, horses, mountain bikes, and motorcycles), traffic is very light to moderate. During Memorial Day weekend, we encountered no more than eleven people, most of whom were within 2 miles of the trailhead.

Trailhead Access

Take the Nevada Avenue exit from I-25 and head south. Turn right (west) on Cheyene Boulevard and continue into North Cheyenne Canyon Park. At the end of the park, continue on High Drive (one-way gravel road) approximately 1.4 miles to the obvious trailhead at a parking area.

Trail Description

With few intersections, the Jones Park Trail (667) is an easy trail to follow. Head west up the trail from the parking area, and follow the trail until it

Jones Park Trail

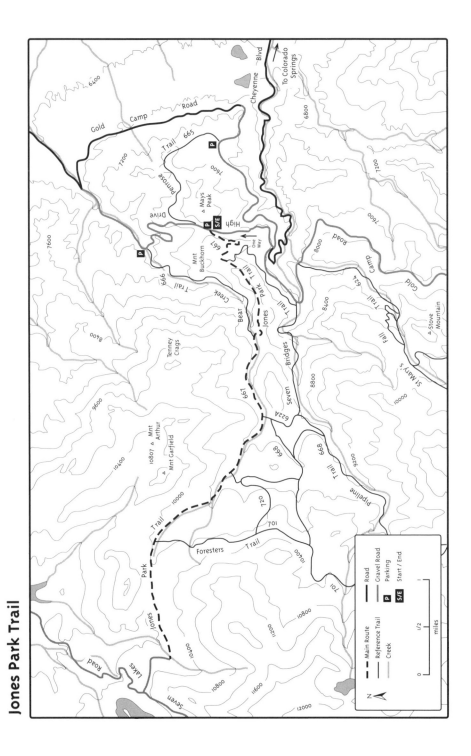

> ### The "Norm"al Guy Says
> "All the loose gravel and sand makes it easy to keep up on the uphills and makes the downhills more than exciting."

reaches South Ruxton Creek and a four-wheel-drive road. The trails are fairly well marked at the major intersections with the trail numbers (not names). Several secondary trails created by motorcyclists exist past the intersection with trail 668 (Pipeline Trail) and 622A (Seven Bridges Trail). Most of the secondary trails rejoin the main trail fairly quickly. When in doubt, follow the older, more established trail that parallels the creek. At the fork in the creek, follow the obvious trail that is on the north side of the right-hand fork. When you reach the Seven Lakes Road spur, turn around and follow Jones Park Trail back to the parking lot.

Alternative Route

On the return leg, at the intersection with 668 and 622A, follow 622A (Seven Bridges Trail) back (east) until it intersects with High Drive. Seven Bridges Trail then climbs up Mount Buckhorn as it parallels High Drive until in intersects with the Jones Park Trail at an unmarked intersection. One

A dog's eye view of Phil Mislinski on the Jones Park Trail.

word of warning: At the intersection of 667 (Jones Park Trail), 668 (Pipeline Trail), and 622A (Seven Bridges Trail), the signs do not say 622A immediately; they say 668. Veer left toward the south and east at each intersection until you begin to see 622A signs.

Trail Notes

- Light horse, bike, motorcycle, and foot traffic
- Dogs must be under voice and sight control
- Water available in the canyon park
- No fee charged

Waldo Canyon Loop

—Monique Cole

A single-track lollipop loop that cuts through a geological layer cake with panoramic views of Pikes Peak and long gradual climbs/descents.

Time: 1.0–2.0 hours
Distance: 7 miles
Start & End Elevation: 7,040 feet
Total Elevation Gain: 1,680 feet
High Point: 8,320 feet
Low Point: 7,040 feet
Best Season: Late spring
    through fall
Support Points: None
Runability: 100%
Difficulty: Easy to moderate
Type: Lollipop loop
Map: Trails Illustrated Number 137
Contact: Pike National Forest Rangers, 719-636-1602

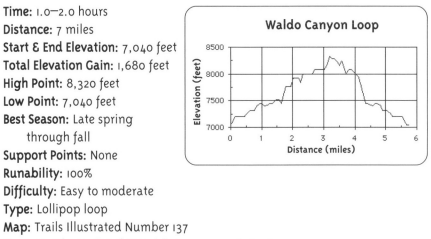

About the Trail

This scenic trail starts just off of Hwy. 24 near Manitou Springs. As it climbs and descends gradually, it cuts through four stratigraphic layers stacked on top of each other. You can watch the rock change under your feet from Pikes Peak granite to sandstone, limestone, and dolomite while interpretive signs describe the geological processes that shaped the area. The majority of this single-track trail is smooth packed dirt and sand covered with gravel from eroding granite. Your speed will be slowed only slightly by a handful of stream crossings, root- and rock-strewn sections, and tight squeezes through coarse boulders that will give your legs a free shave if you're not careful. On

Flowers and storm clouds along the Waldo Canyon Trail. Photo by Monique Cole.

Waldo Canyon Loop

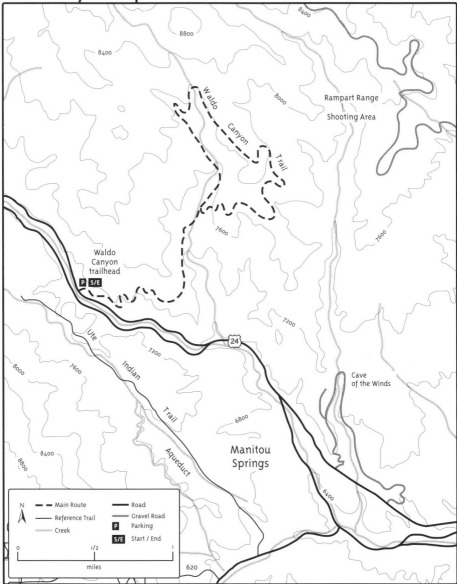

8400

8800

8400

Waldo

Canyon

Trail

8000

Rampart Range
Shooting Area

7600

7600

Waldo
Canyon
trailhead

P S/E

7600

Ute

Indian

7200

Trail

7200

24

7200

Cave
of the Winds

Aqueduct

6800

Manitou
Springs

6400

8000

7600

8400

8800

N

─ ─ ─ Main Route
──── Reference Trail
······ Creek

──── Road
▒▒▒▒ Gravel Road
P Parking
S/E Start / End

0   1/2

miles

620

> ### The "Norm"al Guy Says
> "I wish I had paid attention in geology class."

the north side of the loop, Pikes Peak rears up from behind the mixed pine forest to dominate the landscape.

Trailhead Access

Head west from Manitou Springs on Hwy. 24 about 1.5 miles to the Waldo Canyon trailhead parking lot on the right (north).

Trail Description

This is a very easy trail to follow. At the trailhead, you will ascend a short but steep flight of wood steps, then head roughly east parallel to Hwy. 24. The trail then turns north and drops down to a creek at 2 miles where the 3-mile main loop begins. Turn left to run the loop clockwise for a long, runable climb at the beginning and a fast, switchbacking descent at the end. After closing the loop back down at the creek, turn left to return to the parking lot the way you came.

Trail Notes

- No potable water or toilets at trailhead
- Dogs must be on a leash
- Little or no horse traffic
- Heavy foot and bike traffic on weekends
- No fee charged

Chapter 6
Rocky Mountain National Park & Estes Park

The glacier-carved peaks reflected in pristine high-alpine lakes of Rocky Mountain National Park have attracted mountaineers and nature lovers alike for years. In 1868 famous explorer Maj. John Wesley Powell summited 14,255-foot Longs Peak. And the landscape paintings of Albert Bierstadt in the early 1900s helped to popularize the area.

Now, Rocky Mountain National Park is the most popular attraction in the state with three million visitors per year. But rangers estimate that 85 to 95 percent of those people see the park through their car window, so there is still plenty of elbow room on the trails. Head out early; frequent summer traffic jams are caused by elk-watching tourists and cars flocking to Trail Ridge Road, the highest continuous highway in the country that crosses the divide at 12,183 feet.

Longs Peak dominates the landscape of Rocky Mountain National Park with its towering 14,255 feet. The Diamond, an impressive 1,000-foot vertical rock face on its eastern flank, is Colorado's answer to Yosemite's El Capitan. There are also seventy-seven other peaks over 12,000 feet in the park and countless glacier-fed lakes, ponds, creeks, and waterfalls.

Humans share the park with black bears, mountain lions, bighorn sheep, beavers, otters, bald and golden eagles, hawks, falcons, deer, and the very visible and seasonally audible elk herds. In fall, when an elk bull's fancy turns to mating, their bugling calls can be heard throughout the park's lower meadows. At times the elk are so loud they can be heard high on the wall of the Diamond. The elk herds often wander into Estes Park, the gateway town to Rocky Mountain National Park.

F. O. Stanley, inventor of the Stanley Steamer, fell in love with Estes Park, attributing his recovery from tuberculosis to the clean, dry air. He spearheaded the effort to reintroduce elk to the area and built the stately Stanley Hotel in 1909, transporting hundreds of guests each summer from the Lyons depot via his Stanley Steamer Mountain Wagons. The Stanley Hotel still sits as an elegant sentinel overlooking downtown Estes Park, which has sadly become a crowded conglomeration of souvenir shops, saltwater taffy stores, and other tourist traps.

Après-Run

Estes Park is not exactly the gastronomic capital of Colorado, but you can find decent, inexpensive food and good

Snow resisting spring melt on an early June run on the Loch Vale Trail.

beer at Ed's Cantina & Grill, 362 E. Elkhorn Avenue, and the Estes Park Brewery. The Notchtop Baked Goods & Natural Foods Cafe in the Upper Stanley Village shopping center has microbrews on tap and a healthy menu for breakfast, lunch, and dinner.

Camping may be your best bet for overnights in Rocky Mountain National Park where million-dollar views come at a very low price. You can make advance reservations for Moraine Park and Glacier Basin Campgrounds by calling 800-365-CAMP. Other campgrounds are first-come, first-serve. Permits are required for backcountry camping; call the Backcountry Office at 970-586-1242 for reservations and information. Campgrounds in the national park fill up in the summer, so you may want to check out the Olive Ridge Campground in nearby Roosevelt National Forest (call 800-280-CAMP for reservations).

Abundant cottages, inns, motels, and hotels are also available in Estes Park and surrounding areas—call the Chamber of Commerce at 800-44-ESTES or 970-586-4431. If you want to stay in the hotel that inspired Stephen King to write his best-selling thriller, *The Shining,* check out the historic Stanley Hotel at 800-976-1377 or 970-586-3371.

Resources

Rocky Mountain National Park Headquarters Visitor's Center, Highway 36, Estes Park, CO 80517-8397; 970-586-1206

Estes Park Chamber of Commerce & Visitor's Center, 500 Big Thompson Avenue, Estes Park, CO 80517; 800-44-ESTES or 970-586-4431

Loch Vale Trail

—Phil Mislinski

A gently to moderately climbing single track next to a sometimes raging creek. This trail also passes by pristine alpine lakes and monumental rock formations.

Time: 1.5–2.5 hours
Distance: 6.8 miles
Start & End Elevation: 8,900 feet
Total Elevation Gain: 2,100 feet
High Point: 10,840 feet
Low Point: 8,900 feet
Best Season: Midsummer
    through early fall
Support Points: None
Runability: 90–100%
Difficulty: Moderate
Type: Out-and-Back
Map: Trails Illustrated Number 200
Contact: Rocky Mountain National Park Headquarters, 970-586-1206

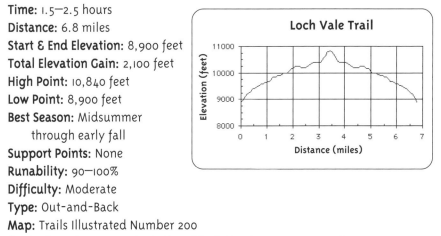

About the Trail

Starting at the Glacier Gorge Trailhead, this run at first seems like one worth skipping. The lower part of the trail is usually congested with slow-moving tourists, but stick with it. After reaching Alberta Falls (well worth seeing) 0.6 mile into the run, the number of people drops off exponentially. The remaining 90 percent of the run takes you by The Loch, Embryo Lake, Timberline Falls, the Cathedral Spires, and ends at Glass Lake. Along the way you will see famous rock formations such as the Petite Grepon and The Sharkstooth.

Trailhead Access

Enter Rocky Mountain National Park at the Beaver Meadows entrance, then turn left onto Bear Lake Road. Park in the switchback parking lot 8.2 miles down Bear Lake Road (Glacier Gorge trailhead).

Trail Description

All of the intersections are well marked, so this is a very easy route to follow. Head south/southeast up the Glacier Gorge Trail to Alberta Falls, then continue past the intersection with the North Longs Peak Trail. Veer right at the next intersection toward Loch Vale. Follow the trail around the west side of The Loch, then continue past the next trail intersection, Embryo Lake, and Timberline Falls, until you reach Glass Lake. If you want to push

Loch Vale Trail

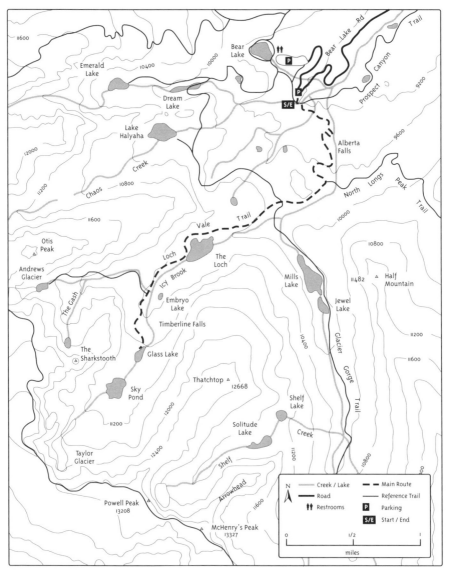

the run another 15 minutes up, follow the unmarked trail around the west side of Glass Lake until you reach Sky Pond. Return the way you came.

Trail Notes

- Heavy to moderate foot traffic to Alberta Falls
- No bikes allowed
- Outhouses at the trailhead
- Dogs are not allowed
- No potable water
- National park fee charged
- Horses are not allowed past the Loch Vale Trail and Glacier Gorge Trail intersection

Longs Peak Trail
—Scott Boulbol & Phil Mislinski

A high-altitude mountain trail running through a variety of landscapes and climate zones, ending at the top of 14,255-foot Longs Peak.

Time: 3.0–6.0 hours

Distance: 12.5 miles

Start & End Elevation: 9,360 feet

Total Elevation Gain: 4,895 feet

High Point: 14,255 feet

Low Point: 9,360 feet

Best Season: Midsummer through early fall

Support Points: None

Runability: 60–90%

Difficulty: Difficult

Type: Out-and-back

Map: Trails Illustrated Number 200

Contact: Rocky Mountain National Park Headquarters, 970-586-1206

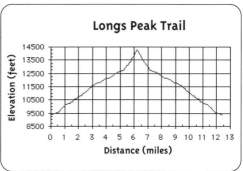

About the Trail

Though this may seem an overwhelming endeavor, Longs Peak is actually quite a runable fourteener, except for the top 2 miles. The beginning of the trail is very steep, but your legs will be fresh, so don't let up. By the time the trail rises above treeline, it has leveled off to a gradual grade. The first half of the trail is smooth and very well kept, but a bit crowded during the summer. Once past the Chasm Lake turnoff, it turns to the northwest and gets a bit rocky, but the masses have usually disappeared. When it reaches the dreaded Boulder Field, the hiking begins. But a fast power hike here is as good as any running workout. From the Keyhole at the top of the Boulder Field, weather turns many runners back. The wind here commonly blows at 50-plus mph. *Do not* attempt to summit if you are not properly equipped. It is still a long way down, and hypothermia can easily set in any time of year. In the late fall and winter months, the lower part of this trail makes a great snowshoe run.

Trailhead Access

Take the Peak to Peak Highway north from Nederland (or south from Estes Park) and turn west at the Longs Peak Trail access road. Park at the main parking lot or on the road between the

Longs Peak Trail

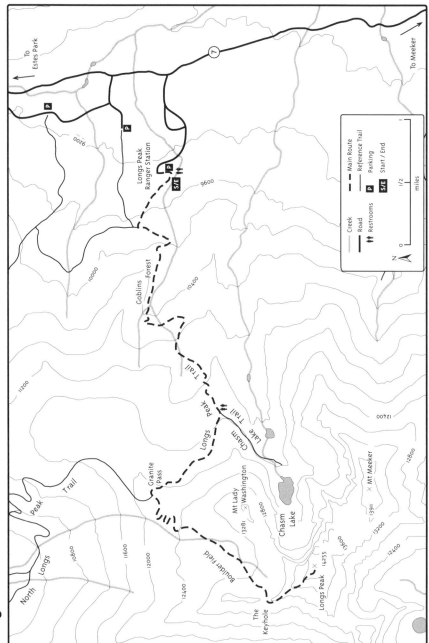

To Estes Park

To Meeker

7

9200

Longs Peak
Ranger Station

S/E

9600

Goblins Forest

10000

10400

11200

Longs Peak Trail

Granite Pass

North Longs Peak Trail

Chasm Lake Trail

12400

Lake Trail

Mt Lady Washington
13281

12800

Chasm Lake

× Mt Meeker

13911

13200

12800

13600

Boulder field

12000

11600

10800

12400

12400

The Keyhole

Longs Peak
14255 ×

Main Route
Reference Trail
Parking
Start / End
Creek
Road
Restrooms

0   1/2   miles

N

The "Norm"al Guy Says

"Hey guys, I think there's a reason they call this a *hiking* trail!"

The sheer rock face of the Diamond provides spectacular views during most of the run up Longs Peak.

lot and the campground to the north. Parking can be full early in the morning during the peak season. The trailhead is next to the ranger station in the parking lot.

Trail Description

Head west onto Longs Peak Trail from the ranger station. Continue along the main trail and cross the footbridge over a cascade. Follow the trail as it winds above treeline. Turn left at the first intersection toward Chasm Lake and climb the switchbacks up to the next intersection. At this intersection turn right toward the Boulder Field and the summit. Traverse across the slope up toward the Boulder Field. At the top of the traverse, turn left at the intersection with the North Longs Peak Trail. Continue up the mountain to the Boulder Field. Once in the field, simply aim at the Keyhole and climb. (The Keyhole is a notch between two large rock formations on the north ridge of the peak. It looks like … well you can guess.) After passing through the Keyhole, turn left and climb the last mile to the summit. (Warning: This section of the trail can be extremely icy and dangerous early and late in the summer.) Don't forget, you need to reverse these instructions to descend back to the parking lot. There are no shortcuts down!

Alternative Route

To shorten this route, simply turn back at Chasm Lake and follow the same route back to the parking area.

Trail Notes

- Heavy to moderate foot traffic in late summer
- No bikes allowed
- Outhouses at the trailhead and below Chasm Lake
- Dogs are not allowed
- No potable water
- Shelters at Chasm Lake and Keyhole
- No fee charged (yet)

(*Note:* This run is *not recommended* for the novice trail runner with little to no backcountry and high-altitude experience.)

Lumpy Ridge Loop
—Phil Mislinski

A fairly rugged loop of moderately rolling to steep single track with great views of the Twin Owls and other rock formations, and a small, scenic high-altitude lake.

Time: 1.75–3.0 hours
Distance: 8.5 miles
Start & End Elevation: 8,160 feet
Total Elevation Gain: 2,220 feet
High Point: 9,120 feet
Low Point: 7,800 feet
Best Season: Late spring through late fall
Support Points: None
Runability: 90–100%
Difficulty: Moderate
Type: Loop
Map: Trails Illustrated Number 200
Contact: Rocky Mountain National Park Headquarters, 970-586-1206

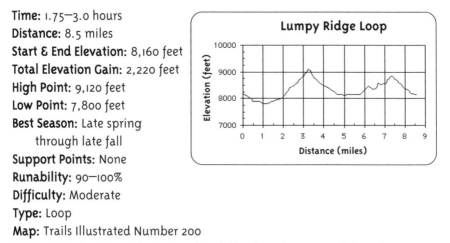

About the Trail

This loop starts from the Twin Owls parking lot just to the north of the historic Stanley Hotel in Estes Park in a lesser-traveled section of Rocky Mountain National Park. As you drive toward the parking lot viewing the Lumpy Ridge rock formations, it will become obvious why it is called Twin Owls. The Twin Owls and the other formations of Lumpy Ridge are so large that they can easily be seen from the summit of Longs Peak to the south. The Lumpy Ridge Loop gives you a much more up-close-and-personal view that is well worth taking. You may want to stop for a quick dip or just to soak in the views at Gem Lake before the steep descent on the way back to the parking lot.

Trailhead Access

Heading west into Estes Park on Hwy. 36, pass the stoplight, then turn right (north) onto MacGregor Avenue (you will pass by the large white Stanley Hotel of Stephen King's *The Shining* fame on your right). Continue straight north by taking the left fork (veering right will take you onto Devil's Gulch Road) past MacGregor Ranch until you reach the Twin Owls parking area. On summer weekends the parking lot fills fast and parking is prohibited along

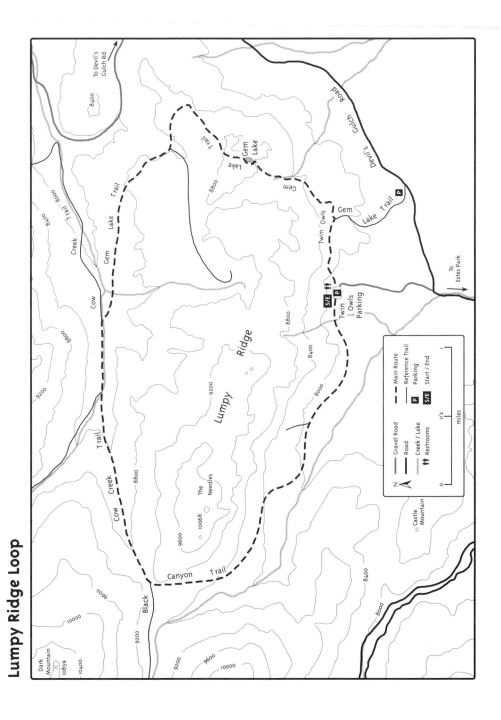

Lumpy Ridge Loop

Rock formations, seen from the trail near Gem Lake.

MacGregor Avenue where it passes through private property. Be prepared to add some distance to your run by parking farther south on MacGregor Avenue.

Trail Description

From the parking lot, head west through the meadow along the base of Lumpy Ridge toward Cow Creek. This trail becomes Black Canyon Trail. Follow the trail as it veers to the north and begins to climb. At the top of the climb, veer to the right (north to northeast) on Cow Creek Trail. Follow the

The "Norm"al Guy Says

"After eating all that fudge and saltwater taffy in Estes Park, this loop made me feel a little lumpy."

sometimes steep single track as it heads down through the forest and enters a meadow. Cross Cow Creek so it is on your right and begin watching for the Gem Lake signs. Turn right and cross the creek again on the Gem Lake Trail—a sign will say To Gem Lake. (*Note:* If you reach several log cabins, you went too far on Cow Creek Trail.) Continue up the Gem Lake Trail until you reach Gem Lake. Pass around the west side of the lake to pick up the trail on the south side of the lake. Continue down the fairly steep trail following the obvious signs back to the Twin Owls parking area.

Alternative Route

Run the loop in the opposite direction.

Trail Notes

- Moderate foot traffic near the trailhead and at Gem Lake
- No bikes allowed
- Outhouses and potable water at the Twin Owls parking area
- Dogs are not allowed
- No fee charged (yet)

Tour de Lakes

—Phil Mislinski

This run is exactly what Rocky Mountain National Park is all about—incredible trails in a pristine high-altitude, backcountry setting.

Time: 2.5–4.0 hours
Distance: 11.1 miles
Start & End Elevation: 8,800 feet
Total Elevation Gain: 3,560 feet
High Point: 10,720 feet
Low Point: 8,320 feet
Best Season: Mid- to late summer
Support Points: None
Runability: 85–95%
Difficulty: Very difficult
Type: Loop
Map: Trails Illustrated Number 200
Contact: Rocky Mountain National Park Headquarters, 970-586-1206

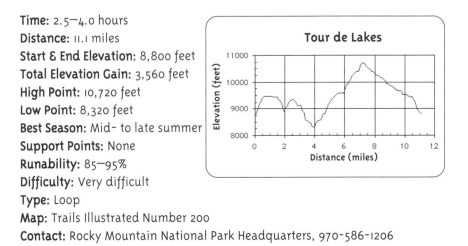

About the Trail

This run captures the complete essence of Rocky Mountain National Park (we don't mean traffic jams of motorhomes filled with bermuda-short and black-knee-high-wearing, Nikon-toting tourists who want to pet the elk). This loop plunges deep into the backcountry, taking you past several pristine lakes and streams, incredible waterfalls, and towering rock formations, including Notch Top Mountain and the Little Matterhorn. Lakes that you will pass include Bierstadt, Cub, Fern, Odessa, Two Rivers, Bear, and several small un-named ponds. The nineteenth-century naturalist painter, Albert Bierstadt, captured much of this area in his paintings. As a result of his work, the first

Beautiful views distract the runner from the switchbacks on the way to Bierstadt Lake.

lake on the tour bears his name. After seeing some of his paintings on exhibit in the National Art Gallery in Washington, D.C., we decided that we had to see the landscape that he found so

Tour de Lakes

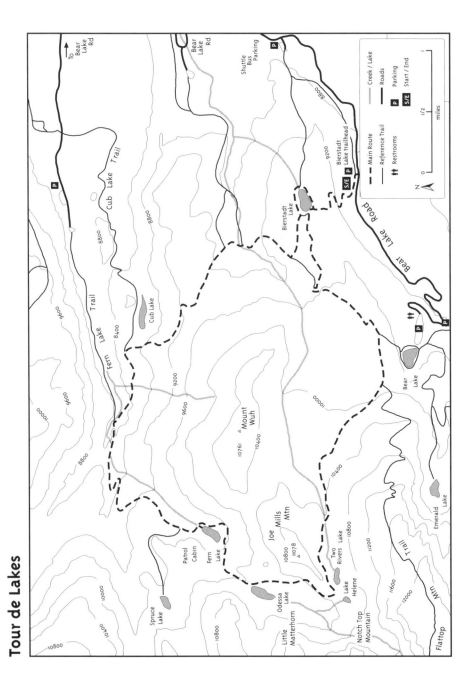

inspirational. This loop did not let us down. It is even more beautiful than we were able to imagine from Albert's breathtaking paintings. This loop makes a great two-day backpacking trip. If you would prefer to do it in this manner, you must obtain a backcountry camping permit. Call the RMNP backcountry office at 970-586-1242 for information.

Trailhead Access

From Estes Park, head west and enter the park at the Beaver Meadows entrance. At the first intersection past the entrance, turn south on Bear Lake Road. Follow the road approximately 6.5 miles to the Bierstadt Lake trailhead on the right.

Trail Description

From the Bierstadt Lake trailhead climb the switchbacking trail up the hill until it levels off. Be sure to enjoy the views of Hallett Peak to the southwest and the upper half of the Diamond on Longs Peak to the southeast as you climb the hillside. After reaching the top of the climb, turn right (northeast) at the marked intersection toward Bierstadt Lake. Follow the trail around the lake to the northern shore. (Option: Take any of the lake access single tracks to the left to get a good view of the lake and Hallett Peak.)

Continue west on the fairly flat single track that runs north of the lake until you reach a T intersection. Turn right (north) at the intersection toward Mills Creek. Follow the trail down a rocky single track and cross Mills Creek

on a two-log bridge. Turn right (north) on the unmarked obvious trail after crossing the creek. (*Note:* There are several campsites in this area so it is easy to miss this trail.) Follow this trail downward with the creek to your right until you pass through a meadow, cross a smaller creek, and reach a marked intersection. Turn left (northwest) toward Cub Lake at this intersection.

Continue on the trail up the gradual to moderate climb, then down a technical downhill to the northwest until you reach a T intersection. Turn left (west) at the intersection toward The Pool and Fern Falls. Continue down to The Pool and Fern Creek (this will be your last downhill for a while).

When you reach The Pool, turn left (west/southwest) onto Fern Lake Trail and begin the climb. Continue up past Fern Falls, then Marguerite Falls (you may hear Margurite Falls, but you won't see them) until you reach Fern Lake. Follow the trail around the northern lip of Fern Lake and cross the bridge at the mouth of the stream coming out of the lake. Be sure to look for rainbow trout hovering near the mouth of the stream.

Follow the trail around the eastern edge of Fern Lake and continue climbing into a talus field. As you get into the talus, you will see the Little

Matterhorn, Notch Top Mountain, and a huge waterfall to the right of the trail. Veer left at the Odessa Lake turnoff toward Bear Lake. Continue on the trail around the southern tip of the large ridge that is to the left (east) of the trail. Follow the trail as it turns to the east and pass Two Rivers Lake, which will be to the right (south).

Pass the Flattop Mountain Trail intersection and continue east toward Bear Lake. When you reach the Bear Lake Trail, veer left (northeast) on the marked trail toward Bierstadt Lake. Turn right (east) at the next marked intersection toward Bierstadt Lake. At the next intersection, head southeast back to your car at the Bierstadt Lake trailhead.

Alternative Routes

It is necessary to use the short access trails to get views of many of the lakes (except Fern and Bierstadt). These short detours are well worth the added run time.

Trail Notes

- Moderate foot traffic near the trailheads
- No bikes allowed
- No dogs allowed
- No potable water
- Fee charged
- Extreme alpine conditions and bad weather may exist at the higher altitudes

(*Note:* This run is *not recommended* for the novice trail runner with little to no back-country and high-altitude experience.)

Chapter 7

Indian Peaks, Winter Park, & the Fraser Valley

Runners from Denver and Boulder looking for high-altitude training often head west to the Fraser Valley and the Indian Peaks Wilderness Area, located on either side of the Continental Divide. Both areas are filled with clear streams, pristine pine forests, and wildflowers that bloom into the late summer along the rolling divide.

Fraser Valley's biggest tourist draw is the Winter Park Ski Area, which is quickly becoming a top summer destination as well, thanks to mountain biking. Some cyclists ride the lifts up the ski mountain to enjoy a free ride downhill while others earn their turns on a 600-mile network of trails in the Fraser Valley. Based on the Adopt a Highway program, local businesses adopt trails, keeping them litter-free and well maintained. And where there are great mountain bike trails, there are great running trails.

Fraser Valley has a diverse history. Once a summer hunting grounds for Ute and Arapaho Indians, trappers followed in search of beaver pelts in the 1820s. Later, Scandinavian loggers arrived along with cattle ranchers. Then came the railroad workers who drilled the 6.2-mile Moffat Tunnel through the Indian Peaks in 1927. Trains still carry skiers from Denver to Winter

Ted Brown, Norm Andrews, and Taz Boulbol enjoy the high-altitude tundra of Indian Peaks. Photo by Scott Boulbol.

Park, and the new Summer Ski Train operates during the resort's popular music festivals.

Black-and-white photos from the 1940s depict chic skiers disembarking from the ski train on their way to one of Colorado's first ski resorts. A simple rope tow was installed on the Denver-owned watershed in 1935, and the ski area is still operated as a nonprofit entity that raises millions of dollars for the city of Denver each year.

Driving north along the curving Hwy. 40 over Berthoud Pass, visitors look down into the scenic Fraser Valley, flanked by peaks rising to 13,000 feet. The valley widens dramatically from its head, where Winter Park is located, into Middle Park. To the east lie the equally beautiful Indian Peaks.

Less crowded than its more famous neighbor to the north, Rocky Mountain National Park, the Indian Peaks Wilderness Area straddles the divide with dozens of beautiful alpine lakes collecting below steep, rugged peaks. And it may be growing. A bill introduced to the legislature by Rep. David Skaggs, D-Colorado, in August of 1998 would add 30,030 acres to the Indian Peaks Wilderness Area. The bill aims to protect big-game migration corridors and old-growth lodgepole pine forests.

Farther east, the Roosevelt National Forest acts as a buffer between the wilderness area and the Peak to Peak Highway, a nationally designated scenic and historic byway. Along the highway, the small towns of Nederland and Ward offer striking contrast to their yuppie neighbor to the east, Boulder. Home to a strange mix of people escaping the crowds of the city, at their post offices born-again hippies rub elbows with militant members of the National Rifle Association. The tempo of life is slow, and for the most part the diverse residents are friendly.

Après-Run—Winter Park & Fraser Valley

Pizza is an art form in Winter Park and Hernando's Pizza Pub has the best of the best (970-726-5409). Located on the main drag near Kings Crossing Center, the healthy and tasty pies, along with pasta and salads, are served at tables encircling a round fireplace. For breakfast or lunch, the locals flock to the Carver Brothers' Bakery for fresh pastries, hearty egg breakfasts, soups, salads, and sandwiches found off the main drag behind Cooper Creek Square (970-726-8202).

The usual ski resort lodges, hotels, and condominiums are of course found in Winter Park (call the Chamber of Commerce listed under Resources for more info). The Morningstar Ranch is a bed and breakfast inn with a secluded forest setting (970-726-4895). Less expensive accommodations can be had farther north along Hwy. 40 near Tabernash. The YMCA Snow Mountain Ranch offers great values from family cabins to dorm-style rooms and even campsites along with an extensive trail system right out the back door. Call 970-887-2152 or in Denver 303-443-4743 for reservations and information.

Within 5 miles of Winter Park, you can camp at the Robbers Roost or Idlewild Campgrounds, both in Arapaho National Forest. Those, as well as Saw Mill and Denver Creek Campgrounds, northwest of Granby, can be reserved by calling 800-280-CAMP. A couple of smaller campgrounds with smaller fees are located in the Fraser Experimental Forest. Backcountry permits are required to camp in the Indian Peaks Wilderness Area and can be acquired (small fee) at the Sulphur Ranger District Office (see Resources).

Resources—Winter Park & Fraser Valley

Winter Park/Fraser Valley Chamber of Commerce, Hwy. 40/P.O. Box

3236, Winter Park, CO 80482; 800-722-4118 (reservations only) or 970-726-4118 or 303-422-0666 Denver direct

Winter Park Central Reservations, 800-453-2525, 970-726-5587, or 303-447-0588 (Denver)

Arapaho National Forest, Sulphur Ranger District Office, 62429 Hwy. 40, Granby, CO 80446; 970-887-4100

Après-Run—Indian Peaks

After a long day running, it's difficult to decide between an enormous calzone with a glass of merlot at Neapolitan's Italian Restaurant in Nederland's Wolf Tongue Square or creative cuisine and a microbrew at the Tungsten Grille on the corner of Peak to Peak and Hwy. 119. For breakfast, try Annie's Cafe & Bakery on Lakeview Drive (next door to the video store) or grab a quick pastry and cup of java at Laura's Mountain Bakery on Hwy. 119 on the east side of town.

In Nederland, accommodations vary from the Nederland International Youth Hostel (303-258-7788) to the Lodge at Nederland (800-279-9463). The Nederhaus and its sister lodge, the Goldminer Inn, are both decorated with antiques (303-258-3585). Originally built in 1897 to accommodate miners, the Goldminer Hotel in the historic town of Eldora has consistently served as a hotel or bed and breakfast ever since.

While Ward has slim pickings for cuisine and lodging, the nearby Gold Lake Mountain Resort & Spa is an oasis of luxury in the mountains (303-459-3544; http://www.goldlake.com). Its romantic log cabins with gas fireplaces, lakeside hot tubs, full-service spa, free recreational equipment, and gourmet restaurant can't be beat.

It's small (only 8 tent sites), without potable water or toilets, and free, but the Buckingham/Fourth of July Campground is fairly close to the Hessie trailhead (from Nederland, head west on CR 130 through the town of Eldora, veering right at the fork after the pavement ends). It is operated by the Boulder Parks and Recreation Department and is first-come, first-serve.

Within Roosevelt National Forest, several campgrounds, including Pawnee, Rainbow Lakes, and Peaceful Valley, are fairly close to trailheads in this chapter. Call 800-280-CAMP for reservations. Backcountry permits are required to camp in the Indian Peaks Wilderness Area and can be acquired (small fee) at the Boulder Ranger District Office (see Resources) and at the Indian Peaks Hardware Store in Nederland.

Resources—Indian Peaks

Indian Peaks Wilderness Area/ Roosevelt National Forest, Boulder Ranger District Office, 2995 Baseline Road, Boulder, CO 80303; 303-444-6600

Nederland Area Chamber of Commerce, Visitor's Center in RTD parking lot on Peak to Peak Highway; 303-258-3936

Berthoud Pass

—*Scott Boulbol*

A high-altitude, out-and-back trail that rolls along the Continental Divide, offering breathtaking views. The trail is mostly single track (some "no track") over runable tundra with limited climbing.

Time: 2.0–2.5 hours
Distance: 7.8 miles
Start & End Elevation: 11,280 feet
Total Elevation Gain: 2,540 feet
High Point: 12,490 feet
Low Point: 11,280 feet
Best Season: Late summer
    to early fall
Support Points: None
Runability: 70–90%
Difficulty: Moderate
Type: Out-and-back
Map: Trails Illustrated Number 103
Contact: Sulphur Ranger District Office, 970-887-4100

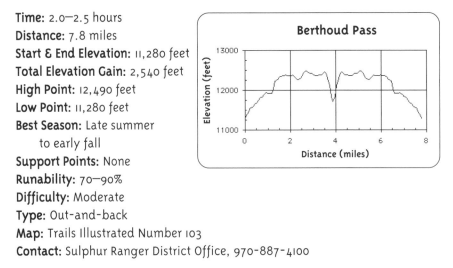

About the Trail

If you've ever wanted to spend a couple of hours running above timberline, but felt too lazy to make the original climb to get there, this trail is perfect. About an hour from Boulder or Denver, this trail offers virtually endless high-altitude running, much of which does not require a massive climb straight up the side of a mountain. There is a steep climb to the first ridge, but it is relatively short and can be run almost the entire way. The short switchbacks near the top offer even the best mountain runners a serious challenge. Once there, the ridge offers miles of tundra, over undulating terrain. We chose to run to Vasquez Pass, at about 11,900 feet, but there are hundreds more miles to run. Some of the trail is not defined, but cairns along the way make it fairly easy to follow. When running the undefined parts of the trail, add rocks to the cairns when possible, to make it easier for future runners to enjoy this trail.

Trailhead Access

From Denver, take I-70 west to I-40 north, (Winter Park exit). Take I-40 all the way up to Berthoud Pass, and park on the west side of the road, just before you reach the lodge at the base of the Berthoud Pass Ski Area. The trailhead is a gated road that leads west up the mountain and is marked as the Continental Divide Trail.

Berthoud Pass

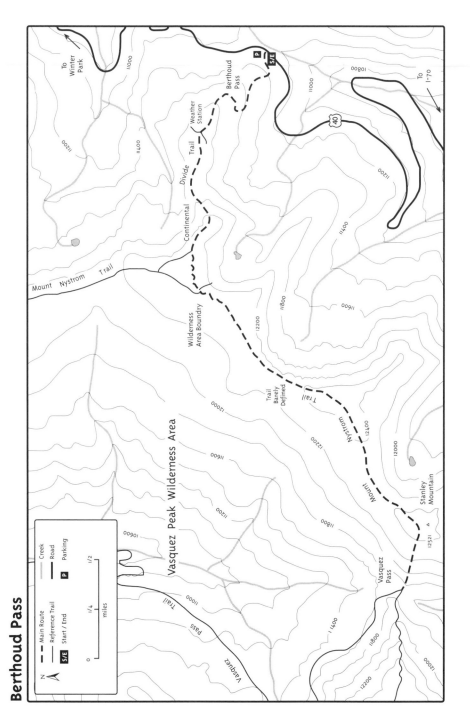

To Winter Park

1000

1100

1200

Continental Divide Trail

Weather Station

Berthoud Pass

P

S/E

10800

11000

40

To I-70

11200

11400

Mount Nystrom Trail

11800

11600

Wilderness Area Boundry

12200

Trail Barely Defined

Nystrom Trail

12400

12000

Stanley Mountain

12521

Mount Nystrom

11800

11600

12000

12200

11200

10600

Vasquez Peak Wilderness Area

Vasquez Pass

Vasquez Pass Trail

1000

1100

11400

11800

12200

12000

Legend:

- – – Main Route
- —— Reference Trail
- S/E Start / End
- Creek
- —— Road
- P Parking

N

0   1/4   1/2
miles

> ### The "Norm"al Guy Says
> "When you guys said this was a breathtaking run, I didn't think you meant literally!!"

Scott Boulbol and Jean-François Lamarque get high on the Continental Divide Trail near Berthoud Pass.

Trail Description

Head west through the gate and climb the service road less than a mile up to the weather station at the first ridge. From there, take the least-defined trail that runs west between the two more clearly defined four-wheel-drive roads. If you start heading downhill, you've made a wrong turn. The trail quickly becomes clear. Follow it across the ridge and to the base of a steep set of short switchbacks. Climb this to the high ridge and turn right at the wilderness area boundary sign. From here the trail follows the ridge southwest through tundra about 2 miles, all the way to the summit of Stanley Mountain, 12,521 feet. The trail then plummets to Vasquez Pass, about 0.5 mile down. Turn back here and retrace the route back to I-40. Many of the sections along the ridge are barely defined, but cairns mark the way. Stay on the trail when it is visible, and take the most direct route between the cairns when the trail is not clear. Vasquez Peak stays within view on the way out, and makes a perfect reference point. It is above the pass to the northwest.

Alternative Route

Lengthen or shorten the run by selecting your own turnaround point.

Trail Notes

- Light foot traffic
- Trail not always clearly marked or obvious
- A leash is required in the wilderness area; dogs must be under voice and sight control at all other times
- Bathrooms and food available at Berthoud Pass Base Lodge
- No bikes allowed
- Little to no horse traffic
- No fee charged

Creekside Loop

—Phil Mislinski

A single-track loop over mostly soft dirt trail through lodgepole pine and aspen groves with an occasional meadow and creek crossing.

Time: 2.0–3.0 hours

Distance: 11 miles

Start & End Elevation: 8,860 feet

Total Elevation Gain: 1,540 feet

High Point: 10,240 feet

Low Point: 8,840 feet

Best Season: Late spring through early fall

Support Points: Aqueduct Road parking area

Runability: 95–100%

Difficulty: Easy

Type: Loop

Map: Trails Illustrated Number 103

Contact: Sulphur Ranger District Office, 970-887-4100

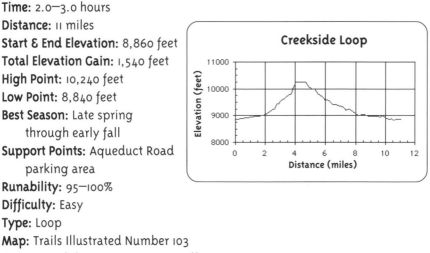

About the Trail

The mountain biking boom in the Winter Park area has created hundreds of miles of new trails, several of which are in the Fraser Experimental Forest. With countless miles of single-track and soft dirt roads, this area is a trail runner's and mountain biker's paradise. Many local businesses have adopted an entire trail or a section of a longer trail and they regularly perform trail maintenance. As a result, most of the trails are well marked and in extremely good shape. The Creekside Loop is a prime example of well-planned and maintained trails. This loop of nontechnical single track on pleasantly soft dirt follows and crosses three separate creeks as it winds through the Fraser Experimental Forest. The Spruce Creek Trail section of the loop provides some moderate to steep climbs and descents. Most of the steeper sections are relatively short and runable. The Creekside and Flume Trails section of the loop is mostly flat to gently rolling single track. If you come across a trail in this area that you absolutely love, be sure to stop by the adopting business and let them know that they are doing a great job.

Trailhead Access

From Hwy. 40 in Fraser, head west on Eisenhower Drive. Take the first left after the railroad tracks onto Leonard

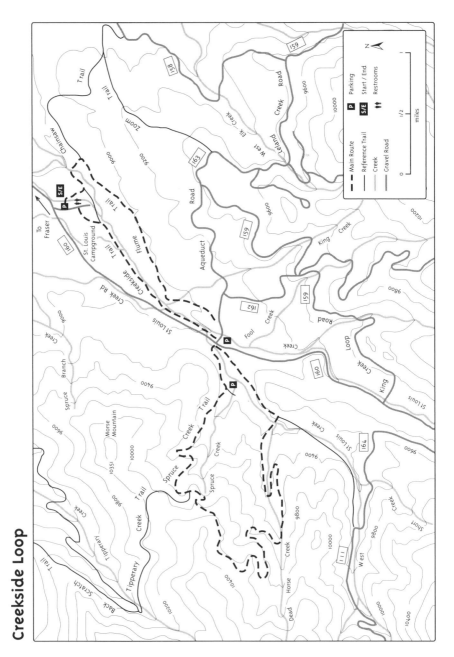

Creekside Loop

Lane. Turn right after a few blocks onto Mill Avenue. This road becomes County Road 73. Continue on County Road 73 for 2.5 miles, then turn left on Road 1601 toward the St. Louis Campground. Park in the open area on the left (there is a mountain bike information bulletin board in the parking area).

Trail Description

From the parking lot, head south on the dirt road, then turn right onto the

> ### The "Norm"al Guy Says
> "This is my kind of area!! I think that I will stop by the pizza place that adopted a trail and get a large pizza and pitcher of beer."

Scenic rest stop on the Creekside Loop.

Creekside Trail. Follow the double-track spur until it joins the main trail. Continue southwest on the Creekside Trail until you reach Aqueduct Road, then turn right. Cross St. Louis Creek Road to pick up the Spruce Creek Trail on the far side. Climb up past the Tipperary Creek Trail intersection and follow the loop as it winds around to Dead Horse Creek then back to St. Louis Creek Road. Cross the road and head southeast on Aqueduct Road. After approximately 0.25 mile, turn left (northeast) onto the Flume Trail. Continue on Flume Trail until you reach the intersection with Chainsaw Trail, then turn left. Cross the creek and take the immediate left onto a double track. After a few hundred yards, turn right onto a single track that takes you back to the parking area (you will be able to see the parking lot through the trees).

Alternative Route

If you only have 45 to 60 minutes to run or don't want to do any climbing, skip the Spruce Creek Trail portion of the loop. Turn left when you reach Aqueduct Road, then take the left onto Flume Trail.

Trail Notes

- Light horse traffic
- Light to moderate bike traffic
- Outhouses at the St. Louis Campground
- No potable water
- No fee charged
- Dogs must be under voice and sight control; a leash should be used near the trailheads and road crossings
- Insect repellent recommended

Hessie to High Lonesome Loop

—Scott Boulbol

A spectacular high-altitude run in the Indian Peaks Wilderness Area, with considerable climbing and descending and a 2-mile stretch along the Continental Divide.

Time: 3.5–5.0 hours
Distance: 14.1 miles
Start & End Elevation: 9,360 feet
Total Elevation Gain: 3,260 feet
High Point: 12,200 feet
Low Point: 9,360 feet
Best Season: Midsummer
    through early fall
Support Points: Rollins Pass Road
Runability: 70–95%
Difficulty: Difficult
Type: Loop
Map: Trails Illustrated Number 103
Contact: Boulder Ranger District Office, 303-444-6600

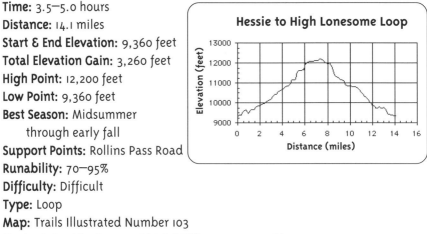

About the Trail

This trail takes the runner along a raging mountain stream, through dense pine forest, above treeline into alpine tundra, and finally up to the Continental Divide. The trail is everything from dirt road to single track to no track (simply follow the string of cairns along the ridge). Offering stunning views of Devil's Thumb, the Arapaho Peaks, Winter Park, and Berthoud Pass, runners will always have something to occupy their oxygen-starved brains. Most years, these trails are only clear of snow from July to October and severe weather is the norm before and after that. During good weather in the winter, however, sections of this loop can make a great snowshoe or ski trail.

Don't be fooled by the distance; this is one of the longest 14.1-mile loops we've run. With the varried terrain and shortage of oxygen, allow at least 3.5 hours to finish.

Trailhead Access

From Nederland, follow Hwy. 119 (Peak to Peak Highway) southwest just out of town and turn right onto 130 Road toward the town of Eldora. Pass the turnoff for the ski area and continue through the town of Eldora, until the road turns to dirt. Continue west about 0.75 mile, then veer left at the fork in the road toward the Hessie Townsite. The road is often covered by a shallow stream, but most cars can make it through. Park at the old townsite just past the stream.

Hessie to High Lonesome Loop

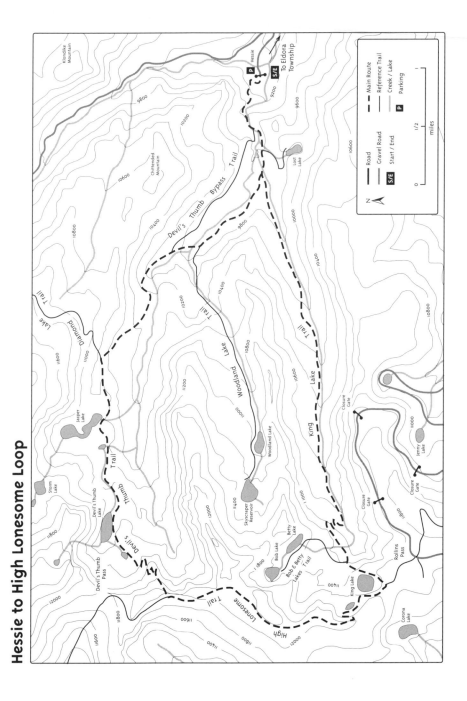

A typical summer day along the King Lake Trail. Photo by Scott Boulbol.

(The road is closed in winter from the end of the pavement.)

Trail Description

From the parking lot, head west along the dirt road across the footbridge. Climb along the rocky road to the second creek crossing. Follow the sign to King Lake Trail and continue heading west until the third crossing. Turn left here and follow the trail about 4 miles to Rollins Pass, just above King Lake. Turn right here to head north on the High Lonesome Trail, also called Continental Divide Trail, to follow the Continental Divide about 2 miles. The trail is faint, but well marked with cairns. The Devil's Thumb Trail con-

> ### The "Norm"al Guy Says
> "I may just drop down from Rollins Pass into Winter Park. They have some great beer down there."

nects with the High Lonesome at the north end of a large saddle (if you start to climb the peak to the north of the saddle, turn back). Two large cairns mark the start of the descent along the Devil's Thumb Trail. Keeping the three lakes to the left, follow this trail downhill, veering left at the Devil's Thumb Bypass Trail, then continue east on the dirt road back to the parking lot.

Alternative Routes

Either King Lake or Devil's Thumb Trail can be run as an out-and-back route, shortening the overall length by a couple miles (or more if you don't complete the trails). Or, run to the Devil's Thumb Trail, turn right, and run about a mile to the intersection of the Woodland Lake Trail on the left. Two miles west, you will pass Woodland Lake and end at Skyscraper Reservoir. Return home on the reverse route for about an 8-mile out-and-back run.

Trail Notes

- Light foot traffic
- Dogs must be on a leash at all times inside wilderness area
- No bathrooms or potable water
- No bikes
- No fee charged

Mount Audubon Trail

—Scott Boulbol

A mostly runable thirteener in the Indian Peaks Wilderness Area, on single track and talus, with incredible views of the surrounding peaks and the Continental Divide.

Time: 2.5_3.5 hours
Distance: 7.8 miles
Start & End Elevation: 10,480 feet
Total Elevation Gain: 2,751 feet
High Point: 13,223
Low Point: 10,480
Best Season: Mid- to late summer
Support Points: None
Runability: 80–90%
Difficulty: Difficult
Type: Out-and-back
Map: Trails Illustrated Number 245
Contact: Boulder Ranger District Office, 303-444-6600

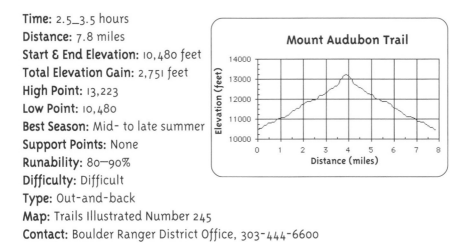

Ted Brown scree-scrambles on the Mount Audubon Trail. Photo by Scott Boulbol.

About the Trail

The Mount Audubon Trail stands out from many other fabulous trails in the Indian Peaks Wilderness Area because this single-track trail offers a thirteener that is almost all runable, thanks to its domelike summit. Any trail at this altitude will present quite a challenge; however, this one is relatively easy because of the gentle grade and relatively short round-trip distance. On one of our research trips up this peak, we brought along our friend Ted who had never even stood above 9,000 feet (1,500 feet lower than the *start* of this trail!). He finished comfortably, but was quite breathless from all his jabbering about the great run. This is an excellent trail for high-altitude train-

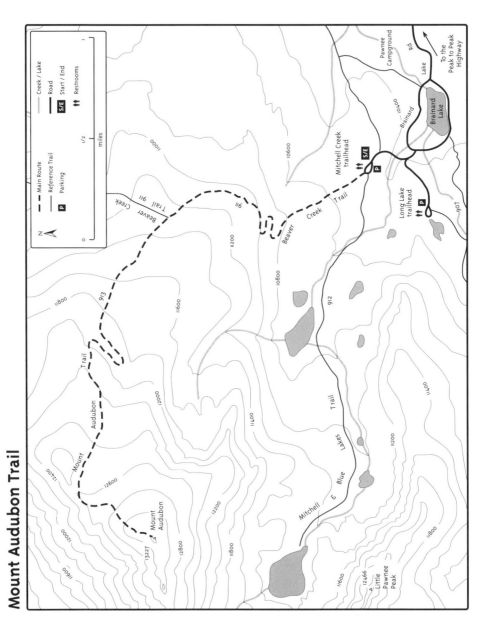

Mount Audubon Trail

ing, as it offers the rare opportunity to actually run above 12,000 feet. Don't turn around when the trail becomes too rough near the summit. The scramble up the last 0.25 mile is an intense aerobic workout and it gets you to the summit views quickly.

The "Norm"al Guy Says

"I could understand being up here if I were an Audubon species, but I'd be flying, not death marching."

Trailhead Access

From Nederland, head north onto the Peak to Peak (Hwy. 72). Continue for 8 miles to the turnoff for Brainard Lake. Turn left and take the road past Brainard Lake and up to the Mitchell Lake trailhead.

Trail Description

From Mitchell Lake parking area take the Beaver Creek Trail north about 1.5 miles, above treeline, until the Mount Audubon Trail intersects to the left. Take this the remaining 2.5 miles to the summit. The last section of talus is only marked with cairns, so follow it carefully. You will be traveling south up the last face, so keep the Front Range foothills to your left and you should be fine. Return the same way as you came up.

Trail Notes

• Light foot traffic
• Dogs allowed: A leash is required at all times
• Bikes not allowed
• Outhouses at the trailhead
• Fee charged

Pawnee Pass

—Scott Boulbol

One of the most scenic runs in the state, this high-altitude out-and-back trail includes wide and narrow single track and some talus. The trail passes two mountain lakes and a waterfall, and tops out above treeline among the Indian Peaks.

Time: 1.5–2.0 hours
Distance: 7.9 miles
Start & End Elevation: 10,540 feet
Total Elevation Gain: 2,020 feet
High Point: 12,560 feet
Low Point: 10,540 feet
Best Season: Midsummer
        to early fall
Support Points: None
Runability: 90–100%
Difficulty: Moderate to difficult
Type: Out-and-back
Map: Trails Illustrated Number 245
Contact: Boulder Ranger District Office, 303-444-6600

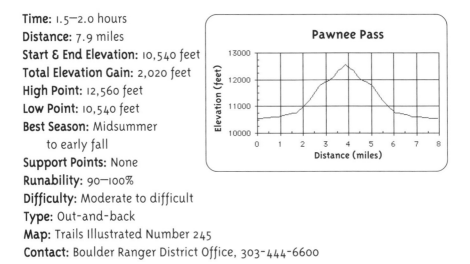

About the Trail

This route offers everything we looked for while researching this book: scenery, runability, accessibility, trail quality, etc. From the start at the Long Lake trailhead in the Brainard Lake Recreation Area, the trail heads west through narrowing forest along South Saint Vrain Creek. It climbs very gradually past Long Lake and then Isabelle Lake, and crosses a natural bridge over a wide waterfall between the two lakes. The trail then heads north above treeline and through the talus along Pawnee Pass. This section of the trail offers incredible views of the lake valley below and the Indian Peaks all around. With the exception of the talus, the trail is very smooth and well maintained. Until the trail turns up the pass, the climb is very gradual. The section before the short climb up to the pass would be a great section to do some high-altitude speed work, although the scenery is so spectacular, speed might be the last thing on your mind.

Trailhead Access

From Nederland head north on Hwy. 72, the Peak to Peak Highway, for 8 miles to the Brainard Lake Recreation Area. Turn left here and continue all the way west to the Long Lake trailhead

Pawnee Pass

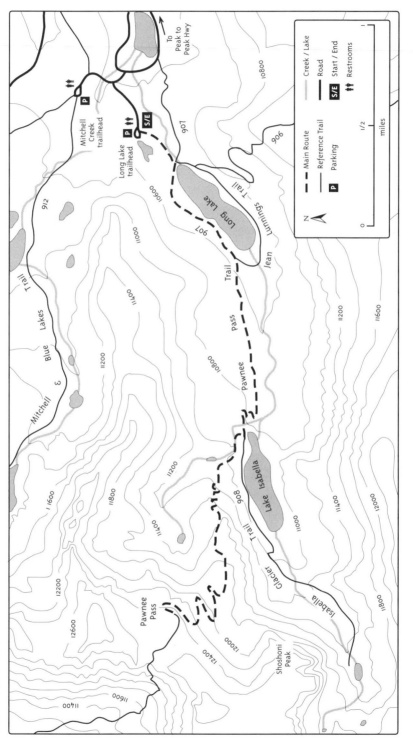

Legend:
- Main Route
- Reference Trail
- P Parking
- Creek / Lake
- Road
- S/E Start / End
- Restrooms

N

0 1/2 miles

Mitchell Creek trailhead

Long Lake trailhead

To Peak to Peak Hwy

907

906

10800

Long Lake

Lumming's Trail

Jean

Pawnee Pass Trail

10600

10000

11400

11200

11600

11200

11400

Mitchell Lakes Trail

Blue

912

Mitchell

3

10800

11800

11400

Lake Isabella

Isabella

808

Glacier Trail

11000

11400

12000

12000

12600

12200

11600

Pawnee Pass

12000

12400

Shoshoni Peak

11800

11200

11600

11400

11700

> ### The "Norm"al Guy Says
> "You guys are right. Sometimes the effort really is worth it."

parking lot, 0.25 mile west of Brainard Lake.

Trail Description

This well-marked trail is extremely easy to follow. From the Long Lake trailhead, take the Long Lake Trail west 0.25 mile to the Pawnee Pass Trail. Continue west to Isabelle Lake and turn north (still on Pawnee Pass Trail) up the switchbacks to the pass. Turn back when the trail starts to descend the other side of the pass toward Blue Lake. Return via the same route.

Alternative Route

For a shorter but still very scenic loop, follow the Pawnee Pass Trail west as above, but turn left onto the Jean Lunning Trail, just before Long Lake. Follow this west around the lake and back to the Pawnee Pass Trail. Turn right and follow this trail back to the parking area.

Shoshoni Peak as seen from the Pawnee Pass Trail. Photo by Scott Boulbol.

Trail Notes

- Moderate to heavy foot traffic
- Dogs must be on a leash at all times
- Outhouses at the trailhead
- No potable water
- No bikes
- Park entry fee

Chapter 8

Summit County

Drivers heading west on I-70 through the Eisenhower Tunnel often have their breath taken away by the awesome beauty of Summit County on the far side. On enormous Dillon Reservoir, white-sailed boats cause ripples to disturb the reflections of snowcapped peaks.

A map of Summit County is almost entirely green, designating national forest and wilderness areas. Except for small corridors around highways and towns, the entire region is set aside for public use. There are four ski areas within Summit County: Breckenridge, Keystone, Arapahoe Basin, and Copper Mountain, all of which become summer playgrounds after the snow melts. All of the resorts have miles of trails open to mountain bikers, hikers, and runners.

The county looked very different when Edna and Max Dercum moved to Dillon in 1942. They remember when Dillon Reservoir was a ranch, and they had to travel all the way to Climax, near Leadville, just to ride a rope tow. Often they would ski in an alpine bowl near their house, which later became Arapahoe Basin Ski Area, thanks to Max's vision. The couple converted their log cabin, built in 1869, into the Ski Tip Lodge, where skiers the likes of Henry Fonda stayed. Later they helped found Loveland Ski Area. Now in their 80s, the Dercums still live in Summit County and still ski. In fact, they both race on the masters circuit, and Edna's latest goal was to teach her great-grandchild Tristan to ski. The couple represent the vibrant life and history of Summit County.

But Summit County's recent history really began in 1859 when prospectors discovered gold on the Upper Blue River. The town originally called "Breckinridge" was established later that year as the first permanent settlement west of Colorado's Continental Divide. Piles of river rock still remain from the decades of dredging on the county's rivers and streams. Breckenridge maintains some of its historical character, especially in the Victorian homes on the south side of Main Street.

The towns of Frisco, Silverthorne, and Dillon ringing the reservoir and close to I-70 are also convenient home bases. Silverthorne is best known for its factory-outlet stores, while Frisco and Dillon both have marinas and a bit more charm. For a great way to spend a morning off from running, rent a boat and fish for trout or just sail on the mountain breezes. Summit County also boasts an incredible paved bike path system that encircles the reservoir and connects Breckenridge and Copper Mountain to the other towns. And, of course, there are miles and miles of mountain biking trails as well.

Mid-August is peak wildflower season south of Eccles Pass near Frisco.

Après-Run

You can still experience a bit of Summit County's history (and perhaps stay in a room where Henry Fonda overnighted) at the Ski Tip Lodge. Eleven rooms are available in the historic building, and breakfast is included. The restaurant also serves lunch and dinner and is considered some of the best dining in Summit County. Call Keystone Central Reservations at 800-222-0188.

For the financially challenged, dormitory-style rooms are offered in a European-style ski lodge in Silverthorne, the Alpine Hutte—call 970-468-6336 for reservations. There's a multitude of other lodging opportunities in this winter and summer playground; call the chamber of commerce and central reservation numbers listed in Resources.

The garlic "mashers" (mashed potatoes) at the Breckenridge Brewery & Pub (600 South Main Street) are unsurpassed. And great views and brews are to be had on the outdoor patio or upstairs dining area. The place really gets hopping at happy hour with pool tables and a busy bar. Really good dinners, house brews, and decent lunches are also to be had at the new Backcountry Brewery (Main Street and Summit Boulevard in Frisco).

The campgrounds in Arapaho National Forest around Dillon Reservoir are jam-packed in the summer, but some sites can be reserved in advance by calling 800-280-CAMP. There are also several campgrounds around Green Mountain Reservoir, 23 miles north of Silverthorne. Call the Dillon Ranger District Office for information on dispersed camping in the forest.

Resources

Arapaho National Forest, Dillon Ranger District Office, 680 Blue River Parkway, Silverthorne, CO 80498; 970-468-5400

Breckenridge Resort Chamber & Central Reservations, 800-221-1091 or 800-800-BREC

Keystone Central Reservations, Box 38, Keystone, CO 80435; 800-222-0188

Lake Dillon Resort Association, 121 Dillon Mall, Suite 102, Dillon, CO 80435; 800-365-6365 or 970-468-6222

Summit County Chamber of Commerce, P.O. Box 214, Frisco, CO 80443; 970-668-0376 or 970-668-5800

Copper Mountain to Breckenridge

—Phil Mislinski

The Wheeler National Recreation Trail is one of the best trails in Summit County. Single track through dense pine forest and high-altitude meadows filled with wildflowers and views from the high ridges of the Tenmile Range make this trail an unforgettable adventure.

Time: 2.0–3.0 hours
Distance: 9.3 miles (one-way)
Start Elevation: 9,680 feet
End Elevation: 9,640 feet
Total Elevation Gain: 2,860 feet
High Point: 12,380 feet
Low Point: 9,640 feet
Best Season: Late summer
    to early fall
Runability: 85–100%
Difficulty: Moderate
Type: One-way with shuttle
Map: Trails Illustrated Numbers 108 and 109
Contact: Arapaho National Forest, Dillon Ranger District Office, 970-468-5400

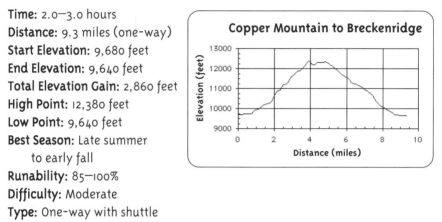

About the Trail

Dennis "The Terminator" Coombs told us that when we were in Summit County we had to go out for beers with him. He didn't tell us which brew pub. All he said was, "Meet me at the Wheeler trailhead near Copper Mountain. Bring your running shoes and beer money."

When we showed up at the trailhead, Dennis pointed to Peaks 7 and 8 and said, "The brew pub is that way, last one there pays." Then Dennis was off faster than a prom dress. Luckily for us the Wheeler National Recreation Trail is far too scenic to run fast.

We caught Dennis near treeline. He was sniffing a few of the millions of wildflowers that line the trail during midsummer. His dog Fletcher was pulling on the leash harder than a rhino in heat. Fletcher obviously had beer on his brain, or at least a doggy biscuit and a bowl of cool water.

Trailhead Access

From I-70 take the Copper Mountain exit (Hwy. 91) and head south. Take the first left toward the gas station and follow the road 0.25 mile to the trailhead parking area.

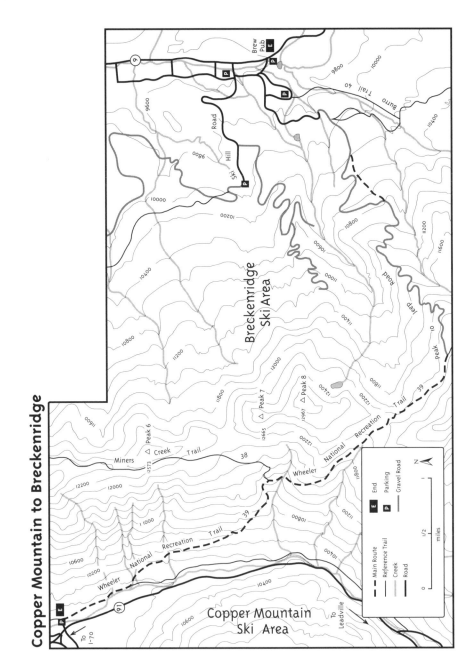

Trail Description

From the parking area, cross the creek, then turn right on the double track (Wheeler Trail). After about a mile, veer left onto the obvious single track to stay on Wheeler Trail and begin the climb. Continue on Wheeler Trail past the intersection with the Miners Creek

Elizabeth Sulzman powers through the flowers on the Wheeler Trail.

Trail until you reach the ridge to the south of Peak 8. Head downhill on the single track and turn left at the intersection with the Peak 10 four-wheel-drive road. Follow the steep and technical four-wheel-drive road to the base of the Breckenridge Ski Area. Keep your eyes open for the cutoff single track on the right it is well worth

> ### The "Norm"al Guy Says
> "I'll drive the shuttle so I can be the first one to the brew pub."

taking. Continue on the Peak 10 Road to the base of the Beaver Run ski lift. Head east on Village Road from the Beaver Run Resort to Main Street in Breckenridge. The Breckenridge Brewery is located at 600 South Main Street on the south end of town.

Alternative Routes

Feel free to take any of the unmarked mountain bike single tracks in the Breckenridge Ski Area. These trails are relatively free of bikers on weekdays. On the weekends you will rarely see bikers riding uphill on these trails; they usually take the ski lifts. Be sure to watch your back for riders.

Trail Notes

- Light foot and bike traffic
- No outhouses or potable water
- Dogs must be on a leash at all times
- No fee charged

Eccles Pass Loop
—Phil Mislinski

A long, high-altitude loop on (mostly) single and double track that takes you deep into the Gore Range.

Time: 3.0–4.5 hours
Distance: 14.5 miles
Start & End Elevation: 9,180 feet
Total Elevation Gain: 3,240 feet
High Point: 11,880 feet
Low Point: 9,180 feet
Best Season: Late summer
to early fall
Support Points: None
Runability: 80–90%
Difficulty: Difficult
Type: Loop
Map: Trails Illustrated Number 108
Contact: Arapaho National Forest, Dillon Ranger District Office, 970-468-5400

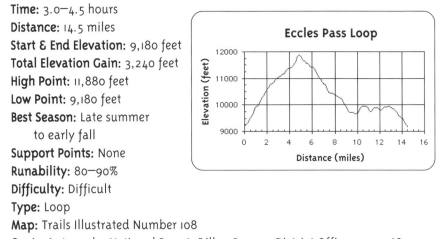

Virgil Best begins the climb to Eccles Pass from the north side on the Gore Range Trail. Photo by Kate Lapides.

About the Trail

Our friends in Breckenridge, Kate and Virgil, said that this is one of their favorite runs in Summit County. After doing the loop, we understood why.

This run is, without a doubt, one of the best in the state. The loop starts by following Meadow Creek through dense forest on the way to the creek's source high above treeline. There are several steep but short climbs early in the run. The effort, however, soon pays off. As the trail reaches treeline, the climb becomes much more gentle as the trail passes through high-alpine meadows filled with wildflowers (thus the name "Meadow" Creek). The slopes of Buffalo Mountain, the rugged peaks of the Gore Range, the notch of Eccles Pass, and the Tenmile Range provide views that are sure to slow the pace. The steep climb to Eccles Pass will also limit your speed. Once over the pass, you then enjoy miles of gradual to steep down-

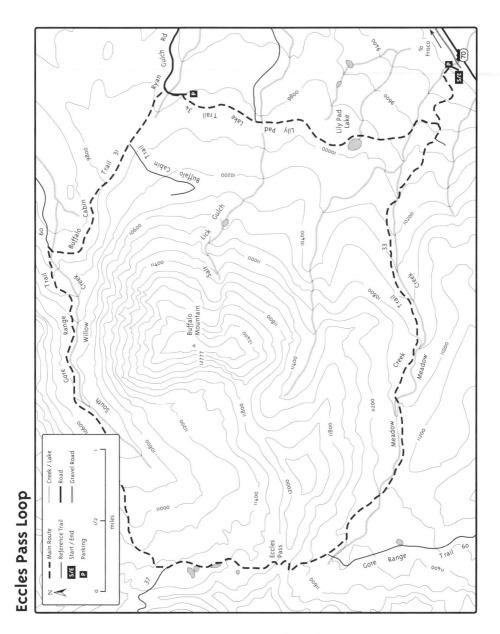

Eccles Pass Loop

hill as you circumnavigate Buffalo Mountain through the narrow and spectacular South Willow Creek Valley. Be sure to stop and enjoy Lily Pad Lake on the north side of Buffalo Mountain before returning to the parking area at the start.

Trailhead Access

Take I-70 to the Frisco/Breckenridge exit (Hwy. 9). Head north (south takes you into Frisco) and take the first left onto the forest access road. Continue approximately 0.5 mile to the parking area.

> ### The "Norm"al Guy Says
> "This run is even better than that brewery run ... except that I have to bring my own beer."

Trail Description

From the parking area, take the Meadow Creek Trail (33) north, then west. Continue past the intersection with the Lily Pad Lake Trail, then take the right fork at an unmarked intersection. Follow the Meadow Creek Trail until you reach the Gore Range Trail. Turn right (north) on the Gore Range Trail (60) and climb over Eccles Pass. After passing several small lakes, veer right at the intersection with the Gore Creek Trail (37) to stay on the Gore Range Trail. After approximately 2 miles, turn right onto the Buffalo Cabin Trail (31). Continue on this trail until you reach Ryan Gulch Road, then turn right, staying on the road a short distance to a parking area. From the parking area at the end of the road, take the Lily Pad Lake Trail (34) south until you reach the intersection with the Meadow Creek Trail. Turn left and follow the switchbacking trail back to the starting point.

Alternative Route

Some people enjoy running the loop in the opposite direction. Either way is a rewarding and beautiful run.

Trail Notes

- Moderate foot traffic
- No facilities
- No potable water
- Dogs must be on a leash at all times
- Bikes are not allowed
- No fee charged

Mesa Cortina to Gore Range

—*Monique Cole*

Fallen logs and stream crossings add interest to this casual out-and-back jaunt through thick aspen and lodgepole pine forests on single- and double-track dirt with views of Mount Buffalo and the Gore Range.

Time: 1.0–1.75 hours
Distance: 8.1 miles
Start & End Elevation: 9,220 feet
Total Elevation Gain: 940 feet
High Point: 9,700 feet
Low Point: 9,160 feet
Best Season: Late spring
through late fall
Runability: 99–100%
Difficulty: Easy
Type: Out-and-back
Map: Trails Illustrated Number 108
Contact: Arapaho National Forest, Dillon Ranger District Office, 970-468-5400

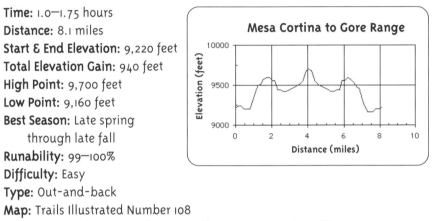

About the Trail

A peaceful atmosphere surrounds this lightly traveled trail that, unlike the majority of Summit County trails, does not go straight up a mountain. Sunlight streams through the quaking aspen leaves while the chirping of birds and the creaking of windblown lodgepole pines may be the only sounds you hear. It's easy to forget you are running, as you climb and descend gradually on a smooth, pine needle–covered dirt trail with nary a stair step in sight. You can practice your hurdling skills while leaping over a dozen fallen pines or your balance-beam skills crossing streams on strategically placed logs (these are two or three logs across, making the crossings easy and safe).

Approaching Buffalo Mountain on the Mesa Cortina Trail. Photo by Monique Cole.

Mesa Cortina to Gore Range

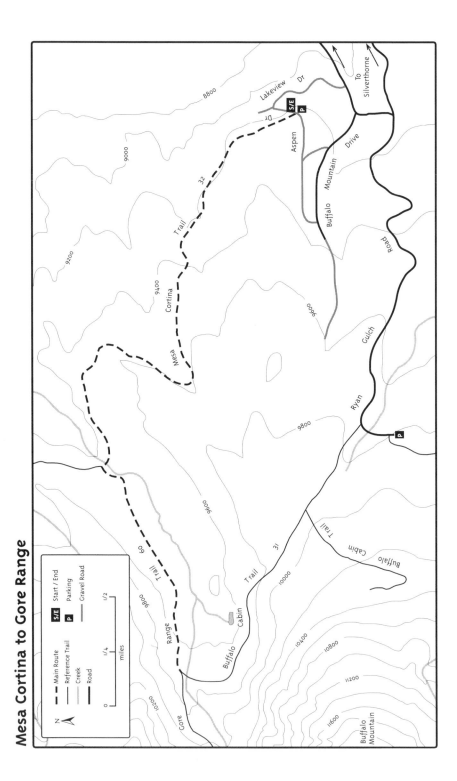

Legend:
- - - Main Route
—— Reference Trail
—— Creek
—— Road
S/E Start / End
P Parking
—— Gravel Road

N

miles

0   1/4   1/2

Occasional glimpses of Dillon Reservoir and great views of Buffalo Mountain and the rugged ridges of the Gore Range at the turnaround are special treats. Most of the trail is in the Eagle's Nest Wilderness Area, so you won't run into any mountain bikers.

Trailhead Access

Take exit 205 from I-70 and head north into Silverthorne. Turn left at the first stoplight onto Wildernest Road. Cross the Blue River, then turn right on Adams Drive and immediately turn left onto Royal Buffalo Drive. After less than a mile, turn right on Lakeview Drive, then after another 0.5 mile, veer left onto Aspen Drive (no street sign). You will see the parking area on your left and the trailhead across the street.

Trail Description

Mesa Cortina and Gore Range Trails are very easy to follow. From the trailhead, run north over rolling slopes on narrow single track through aspen groves and meadows, quickly crossing the Eagle's Nest Wilderness boundary. Then the trail enters a lodgepole pine forest with a few switchbacks (not very steep, but the most climbing you will encounter on the trail). After a marked left turn onto a double-track trail; the Mesa Cortina continues until it crosses South Willow Creek and dead-ends at the Gore Range Trail. After turning left on the Gore Range Trail, you will follow the creek for a while, then climb gradually west (still on double track). Shortly after passing through a big meadow ringed by tall aspen trees, you will come to a signed junction with Mount Buffalo Trail (the Gore Range Trail is called South Willow Creek Trail on this sign). After enjoying the stunning views of Buffalo Mountain and the Gore Range, or dipping your feet in the creek just a short way down Mount Buffalo Trail, turn around and return the way you came, or continue on the alternative route.

Alternative Route

If you continue heading west on Gore Range Trail and veer right onto Gore Creek Trail, you will cross over Red Buffalo Pass and after about 9 additional miles you will eventually reach the Gore Creek Campground, just off of I-70, 5 miles east of Vail. This is a difficult trail through rugged wilderness, so bring extra food, water, clothing, a compass, and a very good topo map. You'll also need someone to pick you up at the Gore Creek Campground.

Trail Notes
• Light foot and horse traffic
• No outhouses or potable water
• Dogs must be on a leash no longer than 6 feet at all times
• No bikes allowed
• No fee charged

Ptarmigan Peak Trail

—Phil Mislinski

Just to the east of Silverthorne, this mostly single-track run provides stunning views of the Gore and Tenmile Ranges as it winds through dense aspen and lodgepole pine forests, topping out well above treeline.

Time: 2.5–3.5 hours
Distance: 11.5 miles
Start & End Elevation: 9,080 feet
Total Elevation Gain: 3,610 feet
High Point: 12,490 feet
Low Point: 9,080 feet
Best Season: Midsummer
   to early fall
Support Points: None
Runability: 90–100%
Difficulty: Moderate to difficult
Type: Out-and-back
Map: Trails Illustrated Number 108
Contact: Arapaho National Forest, Dillon Ranger District Office, 970-468-5400

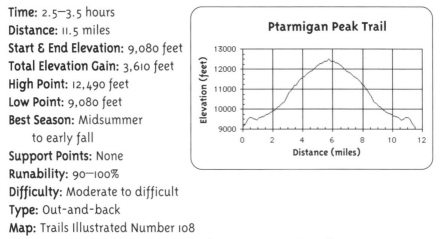

About the Trail

Starting just a few minutes off of I-70 near Silverthorne, this run quickly plunges into the backcountry. After a short but difficult climb, the grade becomes much more gentle as the trail enters one of many aspen groves. Each break in the trees provides increasingly better panoramic views of the Gore Range to the west, the Tenmile Range to the southwest, and Dillon Reservoir to the south. In combination with the single track becoming nicer, the views keep pushing you on to treeline. Late in the summer, the wildflowers make the above-treeline push to the summit much more than just another pleasant high-altitude run. For the last 1.6 miles above treeline, keep your eyes open for the trail's namesake, the ptarmigan. This bird lives in the tundra and its feathers change colors seasonally to blend in with the alpine surroundings. In fall its gray, brown, and black feathers are replaced with white ones in preparation for the coming snows.

Trailhead Access

Take exit 205 from I-70 and head north into Silverthorne. Turn right at the first stoplight onto Rainbow Drive, then take an immediate right onto Tanglewood Lane. Turn right again on Ptarmigan Trail Road and veer right at the sign for the trailhead onto the gravel

Ptarmigan Peak Trail

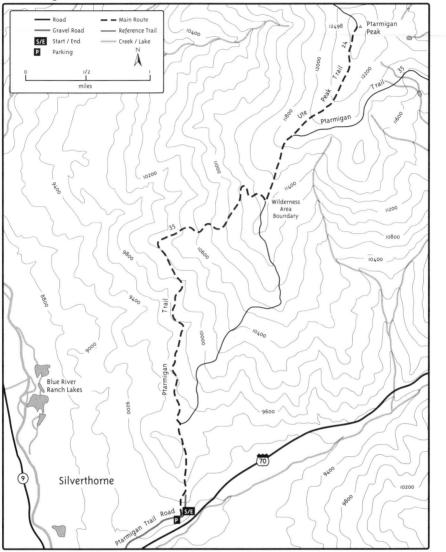

road marked Summit County 2021. The parking area is on the right overlooking Dillon Reservoir, and the trailhead is across the street.

Trail Description

Cross the dirt road from the parking area and pick up the single track. Continue until you reach the dirt road as it winds back around, and turn left on the road. (*Note:* The first 800 feet of trail is on an easement through private property. Stay on the trail and respect the rights of the landowner, otherwise future visitors may not be able to use the trail.) Follow the Trail Easement

Dillon Reservoir ringed by the Tenmile Range as seen from Ptarmigan Peak.

as you pass under the power lines) until you reach the Wilderness Boundary sign above treeline. The Wilderness Boundary sign also marks the other intersection of the two-rut dirt road (now a trail closed to all vehicles). Turn left (north) at the sign and follow the faint double-track trail until you reach the Ute Peak Trail, then veer left on the Ute Peak Trail toward the summit of Ptarmigan Peak. Once you are at the summit, return the way you came for some more great views.

> ### The "Norm"al Guy Says
> "Usually I only get to see the Tenmile Range while I'm skiing. Then the view is a little too close because my face is often planted in the snow."

signposts up the dirt road approximately 100 yards until you reach another single track on the right. Continue on the single track as it climbs up and around the south side of the hill, then enters public land (this is marked with a large sign). Continue up the single track past the two-rut four-wheel-drive road on the right (just

Alternative Routes

You can either go up or come down the old two-rut four-wheel-drive road that is to the east of the Ptarmigan Trail, but at the time of writing, this is not highly recommended. In a few years, trail work may have converted the rugged road to a hiking trail.

Trail Notes
- Light to moderate foot and horse traffic
- No toilets or potable water
- Dogs must be on a leash no longer than 6 feet
- Bikes allowed on trail up to the wilderness area boundary
- No fee charged

Chapter 9

Vail & Leadville

Leadville and Vail may be only 38 miles apart by highway, but they are worlds apart in atmosphere. Leadville's current population is about one-eighth of what it was in 1880, when Leadville was Colorado's second largest city with 24,000 residents. Vail, on the other hand, is a baby of a town, established in 1962.

In Vail, new condominiums, multi-million-dollar homes, and the country's biggest ski area are squeezed into a narrow valley with I-70 bisecting it all. The historic Victorian homes and the abandoned mines of Leadville spread out from Harrison Avenue, the town's main street, with plenty of elbow room in the wide Arkansas Valley flanked by the Sawatch Range to the west and the Mosquito Range to the east.

While other former mining towns in Colorado have sold out to gambling, Leadville retains its historic charm as it struggles to survive on tourism alone. Visitors can still watch a historic melodrama at the Tabor Opera House, built in 1879. One favorite subject is one of the town's tragic figures, Elizabeth "Baby Doe" McCourt. The beautiful young divorcee lured H.A.W. Tabor, Leadville's first millionaire, away from his wife Augusta, creating a scandal equal to the recent Lewinsky-Clinton affair.

Baby Doe became the second Mrs. Tabor, but her husband's fortunes soon declined. When he died penniless, he

Stephanie Ehret climbs her way to a fourth-place finish at the 1998 Leadville Trail 100.

left her the Matchless Mine, believing it would make her rich again someday and asking her to promise she would never sell it. Taking her promise very seriously, Baby Doe became a hermit of sorts, living in a shack near the mine for 36 years until she died of exposure one winter.

While Leadville celebrates its past glory, Vail enjoys present-day glamour. Movie stars and millionaires rub elbows in the restaurants and bars. From early July to early August, premier classical and jazz musicians fill the Vail Valley with music during the Bravo! Colorado festival. In winter, the Bavarian-style village becomes a winter wonderland of beautifully arranged Christmas lights. Vail's shops peddle fur coats and designer sportswear; Leadville's stores sell inexpensive souvenirs and western wear.

But one thing both towns have in common is beautiful mountains and residents who love to play in them. Colorado's two highest peaks, Mt. Elbert (14,433 feet) and Mt. Massive (14,421 feet), dominate Leadville's western view plane. Fisherman ply the waters of the man-made reservoirs of Turquoise Lake and Twin Lakes and the Arkansas River, merely a creek so close to its headwaters. But runners are attracted to the high-altitude trails.

Host to one of the premier 100-mile runs in the country, the Leadville Trail 100, the city is located at 10,152 feet, and the majority of the trails lead up from there. A shorter, but extremely challenging race, the Mosquito Marathon is well worth running. Most of the course is above 12,000 feet, making this race one of the hardest marathons in the country.

At sunset time the rugged ridges of the Gore Range east of Vail erupt with almost volcanic color. The ski town is surrounded by the White River National Forest, and less than 20 miles away are two wilderness areas, Eagles Nest and Holy Cross. With over 100 miles of trails, Holy Cross was once a national monument and is now one of the most used wilderness areas in Colorado. But more and more people are discovering the craggy peaks and wildlife-filled forests of Eagles Nest.

Leadville and Vail share one item of history: the U.S. Army's 10th Mountain Division. During World War II, over 15,000 of these soldiers trained for mountain battle near Leadville at Camp Hale and at the present-day Ski Cooper resort 3 miles away. Each spring a reunion is held at the ski area, while veterans, now in their late 70s and early 80s, wearing their original snow-white camouflage uniforms, ski down the mountain proving they have never lost their love of skiing. The 10th Mountain Division was assigned to the Italian Alps in 1945 and helped secure the liberation of northern Italy. After the war a handful of the mountain troopers became the movers and shakers of Colorado's growing ski industry. One of them, Pete Seibert, along with uranium prospector Earl Eaton, founded the Vail Ski Area.

Après-Run—Leadville

In Leadville, your best bet for good food is the healthy and tasty sandwiches, soups, great coffee, and baked goods (beer on tap, too) at the Cloud City Cafe, 711 Harrison Avenue, or the great Mexican food (beer on tap, too) at The Grill Bar & Cafe at 715 Elm Street.

In the San Isabel National Forest surrounding Leadville, there are hundreds of campsites, including over 350 around Turquoise Lake—call 800-280-CAMP to make reservations. There are also many Victorian homes turned quaint bed and breakfast inns in Leadville along with the historic and elegant Delaware Hotel. Most of the accommodations in Leadville are clean, charming places to stay, but we had a bad cockroach experience at one motel. Contact the chamber of commerce or stop by their visitor's center for referrals and more information on accommodations.

Resources—Leadville

Leadville Ranger District Office, 2015 N. Poplar Street, Leadville, CO 80461; 719-486-0749

Leadville/Lake County Chamber of Commerce, 809 Harrison Avenue, Leadville, CO 80461; 719-486-3900 or 800-933-3901; http://www.colorado.com/leadville

Après-Run—Vail

Vail is the place to push the envelope of your credit-card limit at fine dining establishments like Sweet Basil on E. Gore Creek Drive. You'll find a more casual atmosphere and lower prices at Blu's Beanery on Gore Creek Drive or Pazzo's Pizza with two locations on E. Meadow Drive in Vail and E. Beaver Creek Boulevard in Avon. Also on E. Meadow Drive, the Hubcab offers pub-style dining and great beers brewed on-site.

Give your credit card even more of a workout by staying at one of the area's many luxury hotels like the Vail Cascade (970-476-7111), Hyatt Regency at Beaver Creek (800-233-1234), or the Lodge at Cordillera (800-877-3529). Believe it or not, there is an affordable place to stay right in Vail, too. The Roost Lodge has seventy-two comfortable rooms, a hot tub, and covered pool (970-476-5451).

Minturn, near Vail on the way to Leadville, has a charming, historic small-town feel. The Minturn Inn, a bed and breakfast, holds a special place in Phil's and Monique's hearts as they stayed there on their honeymoon. The young owners have decorated the refurbished 1915 home with beautiful hewn log furniture, and they provide useful advice on trails in the area (800-MINTURN). The Minturn Saloon on Main Street has great barbecue and beers in a lively rustic setting.

For the truly budget conscious, meals cooked over a camp stove and starlit nights in a tent are the best way to go. In White River National Forest, the Gore Creek Campground is the closest to Vail, but a handful of other campgrounds are located within 20 miles. Call 800-280-CAMP for reservations. If you don't mind roughing it a bit, there are beautiful primitive campsites near Piney Lake north of Vail off of Red Sandstone Road. South of Eagle, two beautiful campgrounds are located in the Sylvan Lake State Park. Call 800-678-CAMP or 303-470-1144 in Denver for reservations.

Resources—Vail

Holy Cross Ranger District Office, P.O. Box 190, Minturn, CO 81645; 970-827-5715

Vail Valley Tourism and Convention Bureau; 800-525-3875 or 970-476-1000; http:/www.vailweb.com

Vail/Beaver Creek Reservations, P.O. Box 7, Vail, CO 81658; 800-525-2257 or 970-949-5750

Bed & Breakfast Vail, 800-748-2666

Commando Run

—Scott Boulbol

A spectacular one-way run from the top of Vail Pass to the town of Minturn. Panoramic views abound on this very smooth, mostly single-track and almost all downhill trip along high mountain ridges and through a long creek valley.

Time: 2.5–3.5 hours
Distance: 13.4 miles
Start Elevation: 11,080 feet
End Elevation: 8,000 feet
Total Elevation Gain: 1,260 feet
High Point: 11,680 feet
Low Point: 8,000 feet
Best Season: Late summer
    to early fall
Support Points: None
Runability: 100%
Difficulty: Moderate
Type: One-way (with car shuttle)
Map: Trails Illustrated Numbers 109 and 127
Contact: Holy Cross Ranger District Office, 970-827-5715

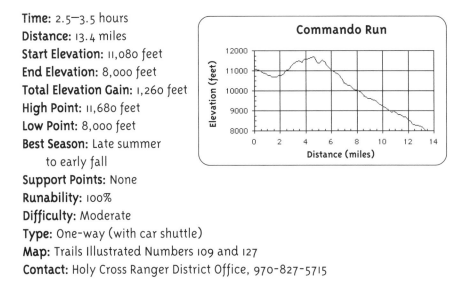

About the Trail

"Wow! Wow! Wow!" This was the bulk of our conversation as we continued along this trail, in the shadow of Mt. Holy Cross, the New York and Gore Ranges, and the high mountain meadows around the Vail Valley. Every ridge offers more fabulous panoramic views than the previous one, and then the trail drops into the valley between Vail Mountain and Super Bowl, soon to be opened to Vail skiers. From here the trail follows Two Elk Creek all the way to the small historic town of Minturn. It truly offers a little of everything, from winding single track through thick forests, to wide open meadows, hair-raising descents, and a gradual cruise along a creek. It even offers a fairly difficult climb, which took us all by surprise. This trail is not quite all downhill, but the climb near the start just makes all the views that much more delicious. Another great attribute of this route is its year-round accessibility. When the snow blankets this area, this becomes a very popular cross-country ski and snowshoe route.

Trailhead Access and Shuttle Directions

Unless you have a chauffeur, the best way to do this route is with two vehicles. From Vail, take both cars west on I-70 to the Minturn exit. Take Hwy.

Commando Run

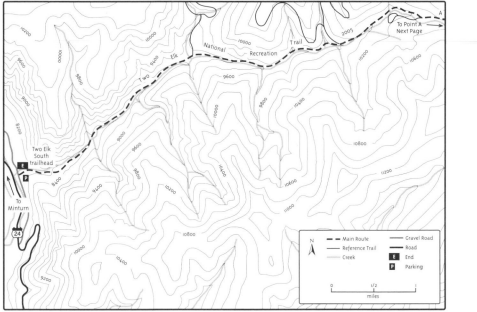

24 south through the town of Minturn. About 0.6 mile from downtown, take a left turn across a bridge over the Eagle River onto Forest Road 762 (unmarked). Take this road south along the river (now on your right) about 2.5 miles, staying right at the first fork, and parking at the second fork. Then take the second car back to I-70. Drive on I-70 east up Vail Pass. At the summit, take the Shrine Pass exit on the right. Turn right and follow signs for Shrine Pass Road. Take Shrine Pass Road 2.5 miles up to the pass. Park in the parking area on the left.

Kurt Blumberg demonstrates running "commando style" on the Commando Trail. Photo by Scott Boulbol.

Trail Description

From the parking area, head west along Shrine Pass Road. Descend about 1.5 miles and turn off Shrine Pass Road, onto the road that forks to the right (from here start to follow signs for the Bowman Shortcut Trail). Run up this road about 0.6 mile and stay left at the

fork. The Bowman Shortcut trailhead is 0.2 mile up on the right. Follow this trail up and down the ridges and across the meadows. A steep descent through a thick forest will lead off the ridge and down to the Two Elk Pass and the intersection of the Two Elk Trail, about 4.5 miles from the trailhead. Turn left onto the Two Elk Trail and head due

Commando Run

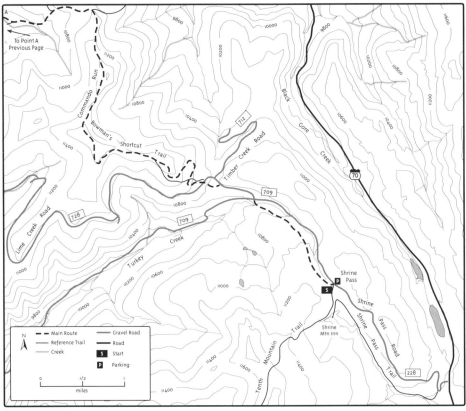

west off the pass toward the Two Elk Creek Valley. The trail follows the creek for about the next 7 miles, and just before the creek empties into the Eagle River, the trail turns right across a footbridge and ends at a parking/camping area. Hopefully your other vehicle will still be there.

Alternative Routes

This route offers two different out-and-back runs, if a shuttle is not available. From Shrine Pass, follow the above directions to Two Elk Pass, and return via the same route, for a hilly but extremely beautiful 2- to 2.5-hour run. Or, start on the Minturn side and run the trail up to Two Elk Pass and

> ### The "Norm"al Guy Says
> "If I could get that heli-ski service to shuttle me up to the ridge above Two Elk Pass, I might just run this route every day."

back. This is a long run, about 16 miles, but offers stunning scenery and only gradual climbing on a very smooth trail.

Trail Notes
- Moderate foot and bike traffic
- Dogs must be under voice and sight control
- Bathrooms at start
- No fee charged

Interlaken Trail

—Phil Mislinski

A gently rolling (virtually flat) single track around the south side of Twin Lakes Reservoir with views of Mount Elbert, Parry Peak, and Twin Peaks.

Time: 2.5–3.5 hours
Distance: 12.8 miles
Start & End Elevation: 9,320 feet
Total Elevation Gain: 1,060 feet
High Point: 9,420 feet
Low Point: 9,200 feet
Best Season: Spring through fall
Support Points: Willis Gulch
    trailhead (turnaround point)
Runability: 100%
Difficulty: Easy
Type: Out-and-back
Map: Trails Illustrated Numbers 109 and 127
Contact: Leadville Ranger District Office, 719-486-0749

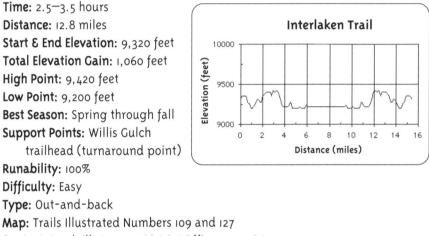

About the Trail

This section of the Colorado Trail is one of the most remarkable because of the smooth, flat terrain and spectacular views of the reservoir, mountains to the west, and the Interlaken ghost town along the way. Starting at the northeast corner of the reservoir, this route follows the shoreline around the south side all the way to the marshy area to the west of the reservoir. The trail stays close to the shore until it reaches the Interlaken Historical Site, a restored ghost town that is well worth strolling around for a while. After leaving Interlaken, the trail plunges into dense aspen and lodgepole forests for a few miles. The shade makes this section of trail great to run on a hot summer day.

At the western end of the run, the trail works its way through the marshy wetlands as it approaches the Willis Gulch trailhead. It is strongly recommended to run this trail first thing in the morning. Not even DDT will keep the mosquitoes away during the late afternoon.

Trailhead Access

From Leadville take Hwy. 24 south for 15 miles to Hwy. 82. Turn right toward Independence Pass on Hwy. 82. After approximately 1.5 miles, park on the left side of the road at the Twin Lakes Dam.

Trail Description

Cross the dam on the gravel road, then veer right on the sandy four-wheel-

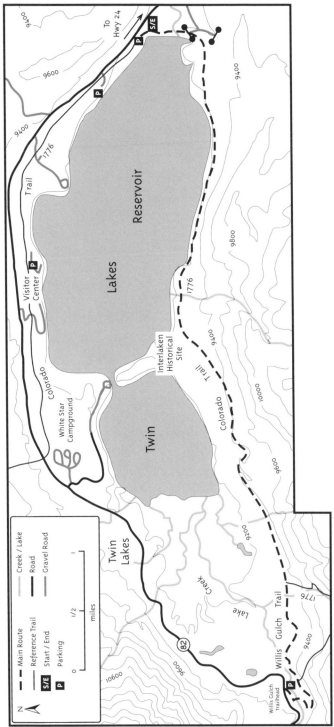

Interlaken Trail

One of the few short climbs on the Interlaken run.

drive road before the second closure gate (the first one is on the dam). Follow the four-wheel-drive road approximately 0.5 mile to the Colorado Trail (1776) trailhead. Follow the single track along the edge of the larger portion of the reservoir until you reach the Interlaken Historical Site. Take time to read the plaques because they provide some interesting history of the area. Continue on the single track as it passes through an open meadow then into the forest. At the intersection marked by a Colorado Trail sign that reads No Vehicles Beyond This Point, and a small Willis Creek sign, veer right toward Willis Creek. Cross several small log bridges over the creeks and one small creek without a bridge. Cross the final large bridge over Lake Creek to enter the Willis Gulch trailhead parking area just off of Hwy. 82. Turn around and go back the way you came or follow the directions in the Alternative Route section.

Alternative Route

If you are the kind of runner who requires a loop to have a sense of closure and you can handle a few miles of road, here is what you do. From the Willis Gulch trailhead, turn right (east) on Hwy. 82 and follow it to the town of Twin Lakes. Continue east out of town on the highway past the White Star Campground. Keep your eyes open for the Colorado Trail as it passes under the highway approximately 0.25 mile to the east of the campground entrance. Scramble down the road embankment to the trail and follow it east along the lake back to the dam.

Trail Notes

- Light to moderate foot and horse traffic
- No toilets or potable water
- Dogs must be on a leash at all times
- Light to moderate mountain bike traffic
- No fee charged

Turquoise Lake

—*Monique Cole*

High altitude with virtually no climbing, this short and scenic exerpt from the Leadville Trail 100 is a great ego boost for the beginner trail runner.

Time: 0.75–1.25 hours
Distance: 7.8 miles (one-way)
Start Elevation: 9,885 feet
End Elevation: 9,880 feet
Total Elevation Gain: 50 feet
High Point: 9,890 feet
Low Point: 9,880 feet
Best Season: Early summer through early fall (snowshoe-friendly in winter)
Support Points: Tabor Boat Ramp
Runability: 100%
Difficulty: Easy
Type: One-way with shuttle
Map: Trails Illustrated Numbers 109 and 126
Contact: Leadville Ranger District Office, 719-486-0749

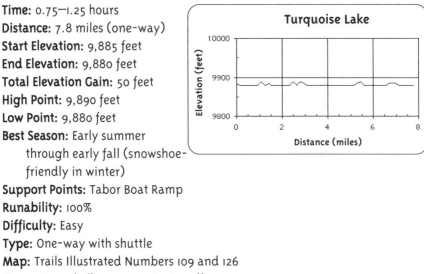

About the Trail

The sun shimmers on the lake, wind-formed ripples lap at the shore, your feet fall quiet on the pine-needle carpet. This trail winds along the northern shore of Turqouise Lake, sometimes coming within inches of the water, then veering away into the pine forest. Except for a few short dips into drainages, the trail is almost level. But you will not get bored, thanks to some twists and turns and a few rocks to remind you that you are, after all, *trail* running. You will also enjoy great views of the towering 14,000-foot peaks around Leadville.

Trailhead Access and Shuttle Directions

From Leadville's main street (Harrison Avenue), turn west on 6th Street. Turn right on McWethey Drive and continue past the Sugar Loafin' Campground. Just after the forest road leading to the Matchless Boat Ramp and just before the dam, a parking lot on the right side of the road is where the trail ends and your shuttle driver should meet you. To get to the trailhead, continue on McWethey Drive over the dam to the May Queen Campground. The trail begins at the end of the campground road on the north side of the lake.

Turquoise Lake

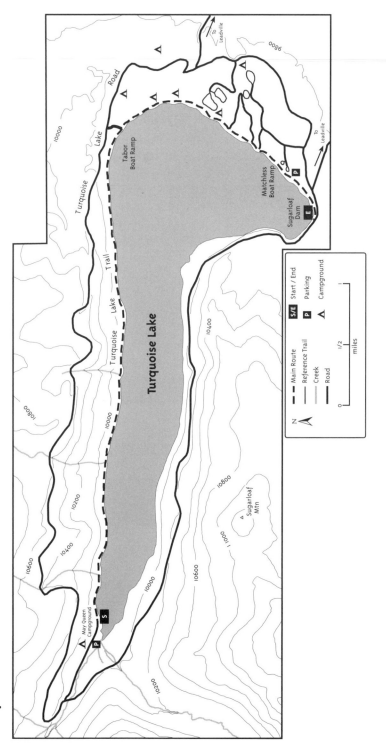

Turquoise Lake

Turquoise Lake Trail

Turquoise Lake Road

Tabor Boat Ramp

Matchless Boat Ramp

Sugarloaf Dam

Sugarloaf Mtn

May Queen Campground

To Leadville

N

Main Route
Reference Trail
Creek
Road

S/E   Start / End
P   Parking
▲   Campground

0   1/2   1
miles

Mount Massive as seen from Turquoise Lake Trail.

The "Norm"al Guy Says

"Very Zen. For once I can enjoy the scenery without worrying about my footwork."

or run back the way you came. If you have a bike, a fun way to avoid excessive driving is to have your friend ride the trail while you run it, and at the dam, switch modes of transportation for the return to May Queen Campground. It would also be entertaining to hitch a ride on a boat back to May Queen.

Trail Description

The trail starts at the turnaround at the edge of the lake. I challenge you to get lost—the trail parallels the shore with the lake always within view to your right. You will pass several campgrounds and picnic areas along the way before reaching the dam at the end of the run. Here you will either be met by a friend

Trail Notes

• Mountain bikes allowed and trail is 100 percent rideable
• Light foot and bike traffic
• Dogs allowed on leash
• Outhouses and potable water at trailhead
• Little to no horse traffic
• No fee charged

Upper Piney River Trail

—Scott Boulbol

An incredibly scenic, high-altitude, single-track run that starts at Piney Lake, above Vail, and follows the valley below the Gore Range, with only light climbing.

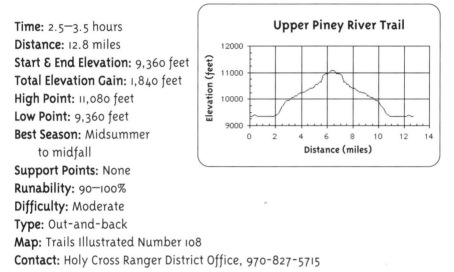

Time: 2.5–3.5 hours
Distance: 12.8 miles
Start & End Elevation: 9,360 feet
Total Elevation Gain: 1,840 feet
High Point: 11,080 feet
Low Point: 9,360 feet
Best Season: Midsummer
   to midfall
Support Points: None
Runability: 90–100%
Difficulty: Moderate
Type: Out-and-back
Map: Trails Illustrated Number 108
Contact: Holy Cross Ranger District Office, 970-827-5715

About the Trail

This is truly a rare find in the high country—a long mountain trail with relatively little climbing. Though the overall altitude gain is over 1,500 feet, most of this is gained in a short, but quite steep, power hike. The majority of this trail is almost flat, making this a relaxing romp through some of the Rockies' most beautiful country. Starting at Piney Lake, itself a reason to make the 13-mile drive up from Vail, this trail goes east along the Upper Piney River. For the first 2 miles or more, there is one giant aspen grove to the north, which was a sea of iridescent gold during our outing. The trail

then starts the main climb, following the cascading creek, and soon levels off in another valley at the base of the Grand Traverse, a string of 13,000-foot peaks that forms the scenic background for the Vail Valley. The trail ends at Upper Piney Lake, which may be even more beautiful than its lower brother.

Trailhead Access

From Vail Village, take the North Frontage Road west to Red Sandstone Road. Make a right and follow Red Sandstone Road to the third switchback, where a left turn will take you onto a dirt road (also called Red Sandstone). Remain on this road about 10

Upper Piney River Trail

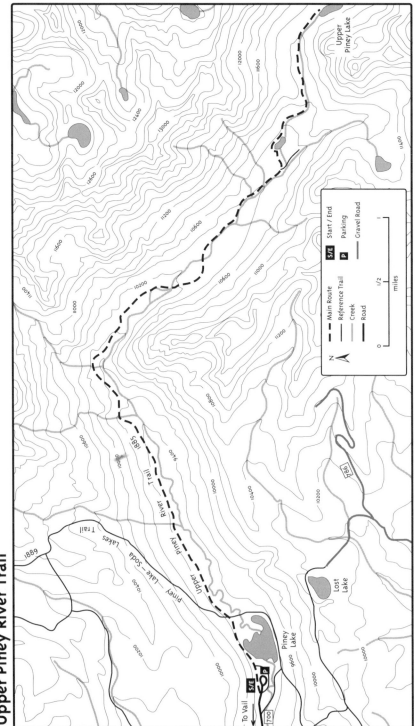

Upper Piney Lake

Upper Piney Lake Trail

Upper Piney River Trail

Piney Lake – Soda Lakes Trail

Lost Lake

Piney Lake

To Vail

N

Main Route	S/E	Start / End
Reference Trail	P	Parking
Creek		Gravel Road
Road		

0   1/2   1

miles

Miles of single track can be found on the Upper Piney River run. Photo by Scott Boulbol.

miles and cross a one-lane wooden bridge, where a sign will direct you to make a right to Piney Lake. Follow this road to the parking lot. The trailhead is straight ahead, just on the north edge of the lake.

Trail Description

Even though this is an out-and-back run, it can be confusing at times because of spur trails that run off the main trail. From the trailhead, run east on the Upper Piney River Trail, passing the Lower Piney Lake on your right. Continue on the Upper Piney River Trail past the intersection with the Piney Lake–Soda Lakes Trail. Once the trail starts to climb along the rocks, next to the cascading creek, there are a couple of social trails alongside the main one. These all lead to the same place, though some are steeper and rockier than others. Later, when the trail levels off in the marsh area below a small lake between the two Piney Lakes, the trail again becomes hard to follow, but the spur trails soon end, while the main trail will continue east. Remember, the trail always remains to the north of the creek, except for a very short stretch at about the 4-mile point.

Alternative Route

Turn back at any point during run.

Trail Notes

- Light foot traffic (except around lower lake where it is heavy)
- Dogs must be on a leash at all times
- Bathrooms at trailhead
- Food and drink sold in summer at the Piney River Ranch at Piney Lake
- Bikes are not allowed
- Horse traffic heavy in area
- No fee charged

Chapter 10

Aspen

Aspen is many things to many people. To skiers and snowboarders, it is one of the best resorts in the country. To superstars and the super-rich, it is a place to escape and/or "be seen." To cultural aficionados, it is a beautiful setting for some of the best musical, dance, and intellectual events in the country. And to outdoor athletes, it is spectacular peaks, glorious wildflowers, and delicious trails.

The town is located in the head of the Roaring Fork Valley. Upstream, the curving, narrow, sometimes hair-raising Hwy. 82 continues above treeline to Independence Pass, offering some of the best roadside scenery in the state. On the other side of the pass, the highway cuts through the town of Twin Lakes near Leadville. Downstream from Aspen, Hwy. 82 parallels the Roaring Fork River as it flows through a broad valley on its way to Glenwood Springs.

Southwest of town, the red striated sandstone of the Maroon Bells, twin peaks each over 14,000 feet, provides striking contrast to the aspen and pine forests below. The image of the Bells reflected in Maroon Lake is one of the most photographed in the state. The area is so popular with hikers that the access road is closed every day between 8:30 A.M. and 5:00 P.M. during the summer, forcing tourists to ride a shuttle bus from town.

It's not unusual to see Aspenites hitting the trails in designer sportswear, expensive jewelry, too much

Aspen offers nearly endless miles of single track for your running pleasure.

makeup, and perfectly coiffed hair. But there are real mountain athletes in Aspen, too, like our friend Neal Beidleman who wrote the foreword to our book and who grew up running and skiing in Aspen.

The original Aspenites were the Ute Indians, who called the area "Shining Mountains." After silver was discovered in 1879, the mining camp was dubbed "Ute City." But that name didn't stick. Instead, the town was called Aspen after the tall, pale, gracefully quaking trees that blanket the mountains in shimmering green by summer and glittering gold in fall. In its heyday, Aspen's population rose to 12,000 residents, who were serviced by six newspapers, two banks, a telephone system, and even electricity.

In 1888 Jerome Wheeler, a silver magnate (and apparent egomaniac), financed the construction of the Wheeler Opera House and the Jerome Hotel. Both buildings became the epicenter of Aspen's cultural life. But in 1893 the demonetization of silver and consequent "silver crash" doomed the town to hard times. Thousands of people lost everything as mines closed and businesses failed.

In 1936, after Aspen's population had declined to about 700, the first ski lift was built on Aspen Mountain. The ten-passenger boat tow cost 10 cents per ride. Today, the world-class ski resort's lift tickets cost almost $60 per day.

In 1947 Aspen experienced a renaissance of sorts, after being discovered by Walter Paepcke, a Chicago industrialist, who was searching for the perfect place for overworked businessmen to revitalize their minds, bodies, and spirits. Following Paepcke's "Aspen Idea," the Music Festival and Aspen Institute were founded, making Aspen into the cultural destination it is today.

With its dedication to fostering understanding between world leaders, the Aspen Institute's summer lecture series has featured such speakers as Margaret Thatcher and George Bush. Restored to their nineteenth-century glory, the Jerome Hotel and Wheeler Opera House remind visitors of Aspen's rich history.

Après-Run

The summer happy hour in Aspen is much more sedate than the glamorous après-ski scene in winter. Children frolic in the water fountain on the downtown mall as tourists slowly walk past upscale shops. The Flying Dog Brew Pub (424 E. Cooper Avenue) with its Hunter S. Thompson–inspired menu, offers great brews like its best-selling "Doggie Style" and a huge variety of food, from cheap pub fare to steak dinners, in a relaxing outdoor setting. The reasonably priced New Mexico–style dinners at La Cocina (308 E. Hopkins Avenue) are favored by locals.

As a world-class resort town, Aspen has a huge variety of luxury accommodations. Our favorite is the Hotel Jerome (800-331-7213), because of its rich and well-preserved history, incredibly friendly service, and modern amenities. For the budget conscious, the St. Moritz Lodge (970-925-3220) offers everything from dormitory-style bunks to private rooms. The "Summer Visitor's Guide," published by the Aspen Chamber Resort Association (see Resources), has a long list of other accommodations.

You can't beat the prices or the views at the campsites near Aspen. There are five national forest campgrounds up Independence Pass Road and several along Maroon Creek Road; some sites can be reserved in advance at 800-280-CAMP. Call the ranger office for more information.

Resources

Aspen Chamber Resort Association, 425 Rio Grande Place, Aspen, CO 81611; 970-925-1940; http://www.aspen.com

Aspen Resort Association Central Reservations, 700 S. Aspen Street, Aspen, CO 81611; 970-925-9000 or 800-262-7736

Aspen Ranger District Office, 806 W. Hallam Street, Aspen, CO 81611; 970-925-3445

Four Passes Loop

—Phil Mislinski

This extremely difficult high-altitude loop encircling the Maroon Bells could be considered the Ultimate Colorado Trail Run.

Time: 6.5–10.0 hours

Distance: 25.6 miles

Start & End Elevation: 9,580 feet

Total Elevation Gain: 7,500 feet

High Point: 12,460 feet

Low Point: 9,580 feet

Best Season: Late summer
through early fall

Support Points: None

Runability: 60–95%

Difficulty: Extremely difficult

Type: Loop

Map: Trails Illustrated Number 128

Contact: Aspen Ranger District Office, 970-925-3445

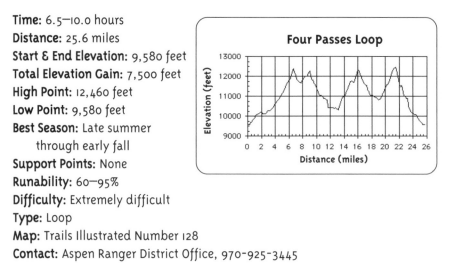

About the Trail

Neal told us that this loop was his favorite trail run in the state and possibly his favorite run anywhere. After putting in hundreds of miles over the summer, we decided that we were fit enough to check it out. Within minutes of leaving the parking lot, we started to agree with Neal. After almost 8 hours of running, we were blown away from both the exertion and the awe. This mammoth loop takes you over four high-altitude passes—all above 12,000 feet—as it circumnavigates the entire Maroon Bells Massive. Along the way you pass through some of the most pristine wilderness that Colorado has to offer. We were overwhelmed by the sheer number of wildflowers (most of which appeared to be on some kind of growth hormone), the constant 360-degree views that make you stop running to take them in, and the almost endless miles of wonderful single track. Our only regret about this run is that humans are not equipped with super wide-angle, panoramic vision eyes. Having six eyes evenly spaced about your head might also be of use, but odds are your brain would seize up from sensory overload. A few words of caution: This run is not meant for the novice or average trail runner. You'd better be in extremely good high-altitude marathon condition before you even think about attempting this loop. There are no aid stations, no sag wagons, and no easy ways out once you commit to finishing the loop. Just because you ran the Denver Marathon in 3 hours or less doesn't necessarily mean that you can finish this loop alive. And remember to bring along a running buddy, plenty of food, extra clothing, and a water-purifying system of some sort.

Trailhead Access

It is *very* important to get an early start for this run. The Maroon Creek Road is closed to incoming traffic from 8:30 A.M. to 5:00 P.M. June through Labor Day and on September weekends. The first bus shuttle leaves Aspen's Ruby Park Transit Center at 9:00 A.M., and the last bus leaves the trailhead at 5:00 P.M., allowing a mere 7 hours to complete the circuit before you are stranded. That said, to drive to the trailhead (leave Aspen at 7:30 A.M. just to be sure), head west on Hwy. 82. About a mile out of town, turn left on Maroon Creek Road. Follow the road about 9 miles until it ends at the parking lot and trailhead near Maroon Lake.

Trail Description

From the parking area, head west on the Maroon Snowmass Trail (1975). Veer left onto the Maroon Lake Scenic Trail, then rejoin the Maroon Snowmass Trail after 0.5 mile. Turn left at the junction with the West Maroon Creek Trail (1970), and head toward Crater Lake. Continue on the West Maroon Creek Trail past all of the campsite trails, Crater Lake, and two creek crossings (the trail picks up directly across the creek both times) until you reach the summit of West Maroon Pass. From the pass, head west on the North Fork Fravert Basin Trail (1974). When you reach an intersection marked only by a very large cairn, turn right to stay on Trail 1974. Continue toward Frigid

> ### The "Norm"al Guy Says
> "No thanks, no thanks, no thanks, no thanks! Those are the only four passes that I will be doing until I get in better shape."

Air Pass past another intersection (this one is marked) until you reach the summit of Frigid Air Pass. Continue on Trail 1974 down into the basin and follow the trail as it parallels the creek. At an intersection marked only by a Campsites Closed for Revegetation sign, turn right and within 0.25 mile, cross the creek. Veer right onto the North Fork Cutoff Trail (1976), toward Trail Rider Pass, and begin climbing. Continue climbing until you reach the intersection with the Geneva Lake Trail (1973), then turn right and climb some more. When you reach a summit ridge near a small pond, continue climbing for another 20 to 30 minutes to reach the top of Trail Rider Pass (don't feel bad, this climb kicked our butts too). From the top of the pass, head down the Geneva Lake Trail where you will see great views of Snowmass Lake until you reach the Maroon Snowmass Trail (1975). Turn right and enjoy the rolling terrain through the dense woods. Cross the creek and begin climbing. Shortly after crossing the creek, you will reach an intersection with a trail that parallels the creek. Even though this looks like a nice trail, it's the wrong way. Take the trail that goes *up*. Continue climbing until you reach the summit of Buckskin Pass. From the top of this pass, head southeast down the extremely technical trail.

Four Passes Loop

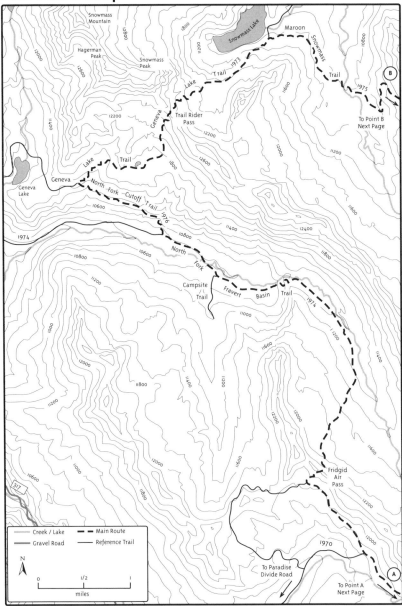

Veer right at the intersection with the Willow Lake Trail to stay on the Maroon Snowmass Trail. Turn left at the intersection with the West Maroon Creek Trail and continue until you reach the parking lot.

Alternative Route

Several people that we ran into along the way said that they prefer to do the loop in the opposite direction. Either way is extremely challenging and rewarding.

Four Passes Loop

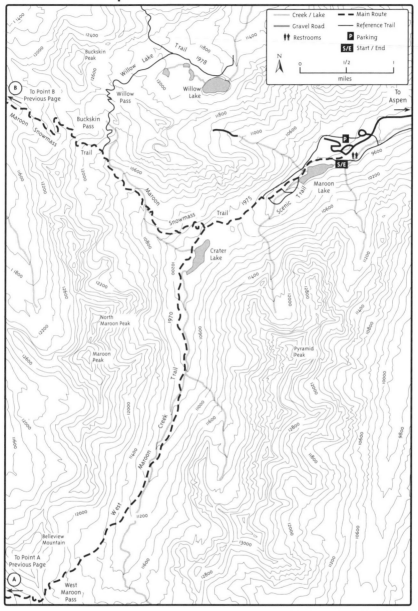

Trail Notes

- Light foot and horse traffic (heavy foot traffic between Maroon and Crater Lakes
- Toilets and potable water at the trailhead
- Dogs must be on a leash at all times
- No bikes allowed
- A water-purification filter and/or iodine tablets are a necessity on this run
- Maroon Creek Road is closed to incoming traffic from 8:30 A.M. to 5:00 P.M., June to Labor Day and on September weekends
- No fee charged

Lost Man Trail

—Monique Cole

An easy high altitude out-and-back with very little climbing through a broad glacial valley along a creek. The single-track trail is very narrow with some rocks and roots to negotiate.

Time: 1.5–2.5 hours
Distance: 7.5 miles
Start & End Elevation: 10,600 feet
Total Elevation Gain: 1,130 feet
High Point: 11,650 feet
Low Point: 10,600 feet
Best Season: Midsummer
through early fall
Support Points: None
Runability: 100%
Difficulty: Easy
Type: Out-and-back
Map: Trails Illustrated Number 127
Contact: Aspen Ranger District Office, 970-925-3445

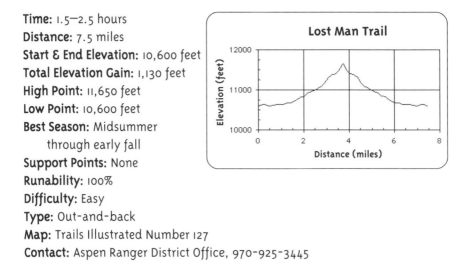

About the Trail

This run is a magical adventure in the Hunter-Fryingpan Wilderness. The trail starts with a quick jaunt to the Lost Man Reservoir, then follows the creek of the same name through a wide U-shaped valley. Most of the run is through riverside shrub lands, with willows, grasses, and wildflowers. At several points along the way, fingers of forest extend into the valley and the trail enters in and out of fragrant conifer forests filled with colorful mushrooms (in late August, at least). Sometimes the creek is lost in the willows; at other times it rushes through big boulders covered with multicolored lichen. Several small creeks run across the trail, most of which are too small to show up on a map. But all the crossings are fairly easy; just hop across the smaller ones or walk across log bridges on the major creeks. The first two-thirds of this trail basically hugs a topographical line, gaining less than 200 feet in 2 miles. After the second major creek crossing, however, it begins to climb toward the junction with South Fork Pass Trail, which is the turnaround point. On the way up, though, you are treated to magnificent above-timberline views of the surrounding 13,000-foot peaks and a gorgeous serrated ridge. This trail is well loved but not loved to death. Painstaking trail work

Lost Man Trail

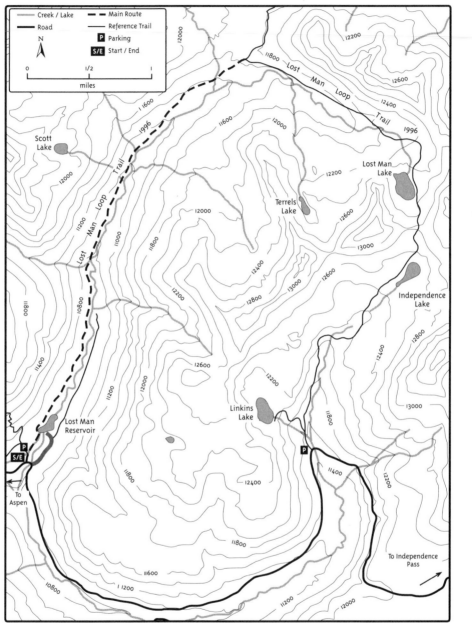

Members of the Aspen High School Cross-Country Team demonstrate that there is much more to being a teenager than playing Nintendo and going to the mall.

The "Norm"al Guy Says

"This is soooo beautiful, and so painless, too!"

has created raised sections with drainage channels in what would otherwise be a boggy mess. This trail can also be a U-shaped one-way route with a car shuttle closing the loop (see Alternative Route).

Trailhead Access

From Aspen, head about 15 miles east up Independence Pass Road (Hwy. 82) to the Lost Man trailhead on the left (north) side of the road.

Trail Description

I challenge anyone, man or woman, to get lost on Lost Man Trail. From the trailhead, follow the sign to the right to get on the Lost Man Trail. After about 100 yards of following a culvert, the trail crosses a dam below Lost Man Reservoir and then takes a sharp right turn to follow the western shore of the reservoir. After passing the reservoir,

the trail parallels the creek for several miles, then veers away from it toward South Fork Pass. At the marked trail junction with South Fork Pass, turn around or follow the directions under Alternative Route.

Alternative Route

This trail is very popular to run as an 8.5-mile loop, but to close the loop you have to arrange a car shuttle or run an extra 4 miles uphill on Independence Pass Road (not recommended because it is very narrow with no shoulders). To get to the trail start, pass the Lost Man trailhead (where your shuttle should meet you later), and continue 4 miles up Independence Pass Road. Look for a parking area on the left at a sharp bend in the road, just before it passes the Roaring Fork River. Follow the Lost Man Loop Trail (1996) north (you'll pass a left-hand fork to Linkins Lake near the start) as it climbs past Independence Lake and Lost Man Lake. Approximately 5 miles from the trailhead, you will reach the junction with the South Fork Pass Trail. Veer left here to stay on the Lost Man Trail (1996) as it descends along Lost Man Creek to the Lost Man trailhead where your shuttle should be waiting for you.

Trail Notes
- Light to moderate foot and horse traffic
- No toilets or potable water
- Dogs must be on a leash at all times; plenty of creeks and lakes for cooling down
- No bikes allowed
- No fee charged

Sunnyside to Hunter Creek Loop

—Phil Mislinski

A challenging loop through immense aspen trees that starts with a very steep, long climb followed by several miles of rolling single track.

Time: 2.0–3.0 hours
Distance: 11.3 miles
Start & End Elevation: 7,800 feet
Total Elevation Gain: 2,540 feet
High Point: 10,080 feet
Low Point: 7,700 feet
Best Season: Late spring
through early fall
Support Points: None
Runability: 80–100%
Difficulty: Moderate to difficult
Type: Loop
Map: Trails Illustrated Number 127
Contact: Aspen Ranger District Office, 970-925-3445

Sunnyside to Hunter Creek Loop

About the Trail

This trail was chosen for the book for two reasons: (1) it is an incredible loop passing through some of the biggest aspen trees in Colorado; (2) it caused Phil to have not only an Elvis sighting, but also a dehydration-induced hallucination involving regurgitated Gummy Bears. (The bears were dancing and talking, so be sure to bring plenty of water.) This route starts with a long, steep climb that has several false summits. In mid- to late summer, the climb up the Sunnyside Trail can be extremely hot and dry, making it even slower. The one good thing about going slower is that you will have plenty of time to enjoy the views of the Aspen Valley to the south and west. At the top, runners are rewarded as the trail enters an old forest with some of the biggest aspen trees in Colorado. Once you reach the Hunter Creek Trail, you will enter a streamside meadow that is often filled with wildflowers (location of the Gummy Bear incident and Elvis sighting). The meadow also contains several log cabins left by early settlers, which are fun to check out. From the meadow you will continue following Hunter Creek as it winds through the trees on its trip down to Aspen where you can pick up the Aspen Bike Path to get back to the starting point.

Trailhead Access

From downtown Aspen, head west on Main Street to Cemetery Lane. Turn right on Cemetery Lane and follow it over the Roaring Fork River, then up the

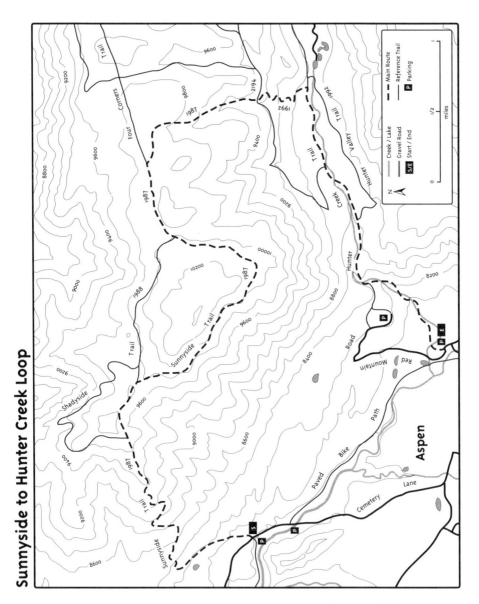

Sunnyside to Hunter Creek Loop

hill for 0.33 mile to the trailhead (on the right) and parking area (on the left).

Trail Description

Cross Cemetery Lane from the parking lot to get to the trailhead and begin climbing Red Mountain on Sunny-side Trail. Continue past the private road

driveways and several false summits into the aspen forest. Pass the first intersection with the Shadyside Trail. Veer right (south) to stay on the Sunny-side Trail at the next intersection with a cutoff to the Shadyside Trail. Continue around the southern side of the summit, then pass the next intersec-

Elizabeth Sulzman and Dennis Coombs in search of Elvis on the Sunnyside Loop.

tion with the Shadyside Trail. Continue east until you reach the next marked intersection, then turn right following Trail 1987 (still the Sunnyside Trail). Head straight through the next intersection (Hunter Creek Trail, 2194) onto the steep switchbacking downhill trail. At the bottom of the hill, turn right (west) onto the Hunter Creek Trail spur. Follow the trail along the creek and through the meadow past the intersection with Hunter Creek Trail (on the right) and Hunter Valley Trail (on the left). Turn left (south) at the next intersection (marked by a Hunter Creek trailhead sign) to cross the creek again. Follow this trail until you hit a residential street and turn right (west) toward Red Mountain Road. Cross Red Mountain Road to pick up the Aspen Bike Path where you turn right. Follow the bike path until it intersects with Cemetery Lane where you turn right to get back to the start.

Alternative Route

Rather than turning right onto Hunter Creek Trail, turn left, then take the first right onto Hunter Valley Trail. Cross the creek, then rejoin the Hunter Creek Trail after about a mile of rambling.

Trail Notes

- Light to moderate foot and horse traffic
- No toilets or potable water
- Dogs must be under voice and sight control at all times
- Light to moderate mountain bike traffic
- No fee charged

Chapter 11

Steamboat Springs

Idyllic alpine scenes are abundant near Steamboat Springs.

Isolated in Colorado's northwest region, Steamboat Springs is a great escape for winter and summer vacationers who want to avoid I-70 traffic. While the area lacks the dramatic peaks and craggy cliffs of other corners of the state, it has its own understated beauty. Aspen, pine, and fir cloak round-topped mountains, meadows bloom thick with wildflowers, streams and brooks cascade through pretty valleys, abundant fish fill alpine lakes, and trails follow the gently rolling Continental Divide.

The town gets its name from a hot springs along the Yampa River that traveling French trappers mistook for the sound of a steamboat. The chugging was silenced, however, in 1908 when railroad workers exploded the rock chamber above the hot springs.

Attracted by great hunting and abundant natural hot springs, north-

ern Utes began summering in Steamboat as far back as the 1300s. Fur trappers came in the 1860s and ranchers followed a decade later. In the 1880s homesteaders flooded the wide Yampa Valley with ranches and farms. Almost simultaneously, a gold strike on Hahns Peak, north of town, brought miners and prospectors to the region. The town of Steamboat Springs itself thrived off the dollars of ranchers, miners, farmers, wounded veterans, and tourists who flocked to the soothing hot springs.

In 1913 Carl Howelsen, a champion ski jumper and cross-country skier from Norway, moved in and forever changed the course of Steamboat's history. The following year, during the town's first Winter Carnival (which he organized), Howelsen wowed the crowd by launching himself over 100 feet in the air off a homemade ski jump. The town still celebrates the Winter Carnival each year with ice sculpture, hockey games, and, of course, ski jumping. By the 1950s Steamboat became a hotbed of downhill skiing and hometown to numerous Olympians. But it wasn't until January of 1963 that the current ski area opened for business.

Although the first homesteader in Steamboat Springs, James Crawford, once counted 150 hot springs in the area, few have survived the town's rapid development. You can still soak away your cares at the Steamboat

Springs Health and Recreation Association and at Strawberry Park Hot Springs (see Après-Run). A self-guided walking tour of seven hot springs takes visitors on a 2-mile trek along the Yampa River, but all the springs are closed to bathing. A map and brochure are available at the Chamber Resort Association (see Resources).

Après-Run

In 1874 James Crawford discovered a hot spring 0.5 mile from his homestead. He dug a hole so his family could enjoy a well-appreciated hot bath and dubbed the spot "Heart Spring." Later, he built a bath house there that was replaced by the swimming and soaking pools at the Steamboat Springs Health and Recreation Association facility, located on the southeast side of town on Lincoln Avenue (Hwy. 40). A more natural soaking experience is found at Strawberry Park Hot Springs, about 8 miles north of town on County Road 36, where small waterfalls link rock-lined soaking pools of varying temperatures.

You can down a "Dog's Breath Brown" on the outdoor patio of the Heavenly Daze Brewery Grill in Ski Time Square at the base of the ski area (closed during mud seasons). But better food and great brews are offered at Steamboat Brewery and Tavern at 5th and Lincoln Avenue. Surprisingly (for a pub), the Tugboat Grill & Pub serves up marvelous omelets (1864 Mount Werner Road).

The number of bed and breakfast inns in Steamboat Springs keeps multiplying. You and your romantic partner can indulge your fantasies by staying in a restored turn-of-the-century church at the Steamboat Bed and Breakfast on Pine Street (970-879-5724). Information on other bed and breakfast inns, large hotels, and condominiums can be acquired from the Chamber Resort Association or Central Reservations (see Resources).

Campsites and rustic cabins are rented at Strawberry Hot Springs (970-879-0342). Incredible campgrounds and dispersed camping is found throughout Routt National Forest, surrounding town. Reservations can be made at least 10 days in advance for several campgrounds by calling 800-280-CAMP. Or check out the campgrounds at three state parks near Steamboat: Pearl Lake, Stagecoach, and Steamboat Lake (call 800-678-2267 or 303-470-1144 to make reservations at least 3 days in advance).

Resources

Routt National Forest, Hahn's Peak Ranger District Office, 57 10th Street, Steamboat Springs, CO 80477; 970-879-1870

Steamboat Springs Chamber Resort Association, 1255 S. Lincoln, Steamboat Springs, CO 80477; 970-879-0880; http://www.steamboat-chamber.com

Steamboat Springs Central Reservations, 1475 Pine Grove Road, Suite 202, Steamboat Springs, CO 80477; 800-922-2722 or 970-879-0740

Fish Creek Falls Trail

—Monique Cole

This out-and-back route feels like a loop thanks to unique views in both directions. The short but difficult climb passes an idyllic waterfall and ends at a beautiful alpine lake.

Time: 2.0–3.5 hours
Distance: 10.6 miles
Start & End Elevation: 7,480 feet
Total Elevation Gain: 2,880 feet
High Point: 9,880 feet
Low Point: 7,400 feet
Best Season: Summer
   through midfall
Support Points: None
Runability: 80–90%
Difficulty: Moderate
Type: Out-and-back
Map: Trails Illustrated Number 118
Contact: Hahn's Peak Ranger District Office, 970-879-1870

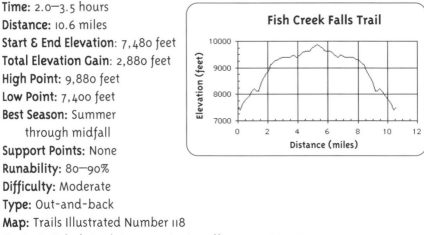

About the Trail

Plunging 283 feet into a pool below, Fish Creek Falls is one of the most popular summer tourist attractions in Steamboat Springs. This trail starts with a view from the base of the falls where tourists gawk and bathers scramble over rocks. The trail then climbs through several different ecosystems. A lush forest of towering aspen, Douglas fir, ferns, and moss provides refreshing shade for the early part of the climb. Unfortunately, other visitors have felt it necessary to carve their initials into the stately and graceful aspen. After crossing Fish Creek on a wood bridge, the trail climbs into the sunny glacier-carved gneiss where sage and juniper

Wildflowers thrive in the mist beside Upper Fish Creek Falls. Photo by Monique Cole.

Fish Creek Falls Trail

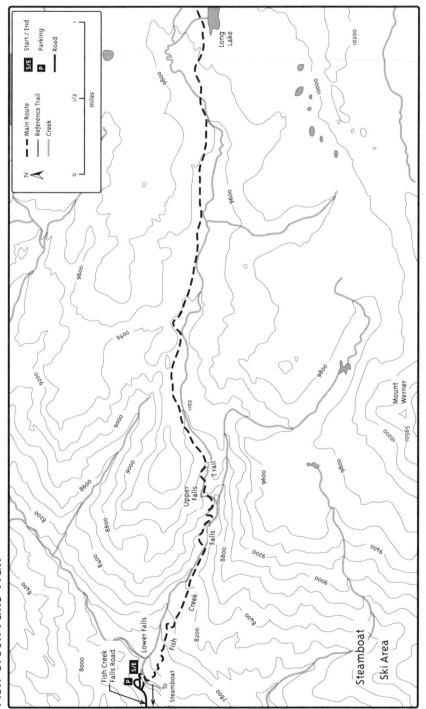

dominate. Cool mist greets you at the small and more secluded upper waterfall—take time to soak your feet or your whole body in the pool before continuing to Long Lake. The return trip offers stunning views of the green pastures and small town of Steamboat below.

Trailhead Access

From Hwy. 40, turn north onto Third Avenue, and continue one block to a four-way stop. Turn right and continue east on Fish Creek Falls Road 4 miles to the day-use parking lot near the trailhead (fee charged). To save a couple bucks, you can park in the overnight lot and run an extra 0.25 mile.

Trail Description

From the parking lot, veer right onto the National Recreation Trail. A short gravel descent will take you to the historic bridge at the base of Fish Creek Falls. Cross the bridge and begin the switchbacking ascent. (Several social trails veer off the main trail for views of the falls.) After crossing another

The "Norm"al Guy Says

"I'm glad I'm confident enough in my masculinity (if not my ankles) to hike on the technical rocky sections."

footbridge, the trail gets hotter, steeper, and more technical as it climbs through glacier-carved rock. You will hear the upper falls before you see it. If you decide to scramble down to the pool, be very careful of your footing as a slip could mean serious injury. After the waterfall, the climb eases off as the trail ascends gently in and out of forests and meadows before reaching the scenic Long Lake. To return, run back the way you came.

Trail Notes

- Moderate to heavy foot traffic
- Dogs must be kept on a leash
- Outhouses and potable water at trailhead
- Bikes allowed, but trail is difficult
- Very light horse traffic
- Fee charged at upper parking lot

Routt Trail

—Phil Mislinski

An extremely smooth and flat section of the Continental Divide Trail through alpine meadows and pine groves.

Time: 2.5–3.5 hours
Distance: 10 miles (one-way)
Start Elevation: 10,040 feet
End Elevation: 10,300 feet
Total Elevation Gain: 1,200 feet
High Point: 10,580 feet
Low Point: 10,000 feet
Best Season: Summer
    through midfall
Support Points: None
Runability: 90–100%
Difficulty: Easy to moderate
Type: One-way with car shuttle
Map: Trails Illustrated Numbers 117 and 118
Contact: Hahn's Peak Ranger District Office, 970-879-1870

About the Trail

This trail is ideal for the novice trail runner who wants to get a taste of high-altitude running without having to spend all day slogging up steep climbs. The trail begins at the base camp parking area and follows the Continental Divide for miles of flat to gently rolling single track. Unlike the Continental Divide Trail in the central and southern parts of Colorado, this section is at or below treeline. It is also very smooth and nontechnical for most of the trip to Buffalo Pass, making it easy to enjoy the scenery rather than watching every step you take. Along the way you encounter several pristine alpine lakes, meadows covered in wildflow-ers, and fairly dense pine forests. It is not uncommon to see deer and elk along the way.

Trailhead Access and Shuttle Directions

From Steamboat, head East on Hwy. 40 up Rabbit Ears Pass. Turn left at the Dumont Lake turnoff. Follow the paved road until it becomes a dirt four-wheel-drive road (Base Camp Road, Forest Road 311). If you don't have a four-wheel-drive vehicle, park here (this will add 4 miles to your run) or follow Base Camp Road 4 miles to the Base Camp parking area. Your shuttle driver should take 36 Road north out

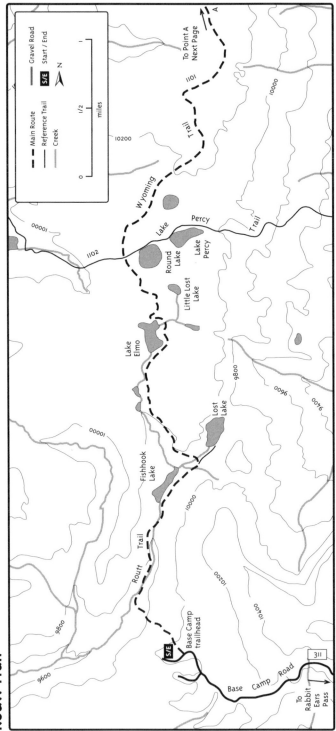

Routt Trail

Routt Trail

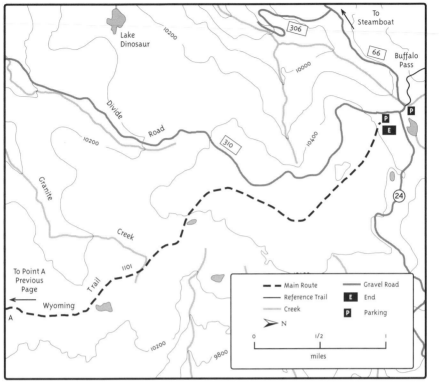

The "Norm"al Guy Says

"I've finally found a section of the Continental Divide Trail that doesn't cause me to see Elvis. The scenery was amazing."

of Steamboat and turn right on 38 Road. Follow 38 Road as it turns north for 1.5 miles to Fire Road 60. Turn right on Fire Road 60 and follow it approximately 10 miles to Buffalo Pass. Turn right on the Divide Road (310), and then immediately turn left into the parking lot.

Trail Description

With few intersections, this trail is relatively easy to follow. Head north on the Routt Trail from the Base Camp parking area and follow the single track as it winds past Fishhook Lake and Lost Lake. There are several fishing access trails that lead to each of the lakes that you pass. Stay on the more worn, obvious trail at these intersections. Continue north past Lake Elmo and Little Lost Lake until you reach the intersection with the Lake Percy Trail (1102) and the Wyoming Trail (1101). A left turn would take you to Long Lake and Fish Creek Falls, and a right turn takes you to Lake Percy. Don't turn; go straight (north) onto the Wyoming Trail. Continue on the Wyoming Trail until you reach a parking area along the Divide Road (310).

Alternative Route

You can do this trail as an out-and-back starting at either end and run as much or as little as you want. The best option is to do a car swap with a friend who starts at the opposite end of the trail (don't forget to get the keys for your friend's car as you pass on the trail).

Trail Notes

- Light to moderate foot traffic
- Dogs must be under voice and sight control at all times; leash required at trailhead and parking area
- No potable water
- Light to moderate mountain bike traffic

One of the many alpine meadows found along the Routt Trail.

- Light horse traffic on weekends
- No fee charged

Chapter 12

Southwestern Colorado

Countless trails, steaming hot springs, towering jagged peaks, cascading waterfalls, and plunging black canyons—Colorado's Southwest is a trail runner's paradise. This part of the state is home to two of Colorado's best ultras, the Hardrock 100 and the Lake City 50, as well as several other great trail races such as the Telluride Get High, the Oh Be Joyful, and the Imogene Pass Trail Race.

Crested Butte is a century-old mining town turned ski town that has not been completely overrun (yet) by celebrities and multimillionaires. It's been called both the wildflower and the mountain bike capital of Colorado, and both abound in the area. Encircling the historic downtown, with its bright, false-fronted businesses, are towering 12,000-foot peaks like Whetstone Mountain, Mt. Axtell, Gothic Mountain, and Mt. Crested Butte itself where the ski area is located. A short distance by trail separates it from its more glamorous neighbor to the north, Aspen, but by road the disparate towns are hours apart.

To the southwest lies Black Canyon country where the Gunnison River has carved a narrow, steep, and deep chasm through stunning black schist and gneiss rock. The most spectacular 12 miles of the 53-mile-long canyon have been set aside as Black Canyon of the Gunnison National Monument. But unfortunately, the trails within the monument are either too short or ill maintained to accommodate runners. Downstream, however, is the still beautiful Gunnison Gorge, a Bureau of Land Management Wilderness Study Area. Gold medal trout fishing attracts sportsmen and the Class III rapids attract boaters, while the scenery along trails like the Ute Trail attracts hikers and runners. But perhaps the best way to enjoy Black Canyon country is to be one of the swifts, golden eagles, red-tailed hawks, or peregrine falcons soaring and diving into its awesome depths.

The wide open spaces surrounding the Black Canyon lie in stark contrast to the steep rock walls, triangular peaks, and serrated ridges of the Uncompahgre Valley. Called the "Switzerland of the Rockies," the mining town of Ouray's Victorian buildings were mostly built before the turn of the century. Now they house hotels, restaurants, shops, theaters, and bed and breakfasts to support the town's new industry: tourism. A soak in one of the many natural hot springs in Ouray and nearby Ridgway is a special treat after running all day in the area's rugged terrain.

Each year, the Imogene Pass run takes almost 1,000 runners and hikers 18 miles from Ouray to Telluride on an eroded four-wheel-drive road. By highway, Telluride is 50 miles away. Nestled into the dead end of a box can-

You don't have to run far from the road to get great views like the Painted Wall within the Black Canyon of the Gunnison National Monument.

yon, the town is surrounded by 13,000-foot peaks, and towering above them all is Mt. Sneffels at 14,158 feet. Like Crested Butte, it is also a mining town turned ski town fending off "Aspenization." In summer, Telluride still has a small-town feel, especially during its annual July 4th parade in which apparently every resident and his dog participates. Summer tourism is boosted by the popular Bluegrass, Wild Mushroom, Film, Jazz, and Hang Gliding Festivals. But the beautiful mountains and spectacular waterfalls are the main attractions.

While we'd rather view scenery from a trail than from a road, the views of the mountains along the winding Hwy. 550 between Ouray and Durango

are unsurpassed. High-alpine peaks give way to red sandstone bluffs as you near Durango. Durango is the biggest city in southwestern Colorado, but is still no bustling metropolis. The historic district along Main Avenue retains a nineteenth-century charm, and the Animas River winds its way through the town. Durango locals are fanatic about mountain biking, and many of the country's best off-road cyclists live here.

Note: In the San Juan National Forest and Weminuche Wilderness, wildlife encounters with abundant mountain goats have become somewhat unsettling. Instead of trekking up to 20 miles to natural salt licks, the mountain goats have found sources much closer to home in the form of human urine. Aside from harassing trail users in the act, the goats also tear up fragile tundra vegetation digging for the urine salts. So whenever possible urinate on durable surfaces such as rocks.

Après-Run

Crested Butte
Elk Avenue, Crested Butte's main street, is host to the Bakery Cafe, with great coffee drinks, baked goods, soups, and sandwiches, and to the Idle Spur, where locals go for steaks, nightlife, and beer, brewed on-site.

Ouray
In Ouray, the Silver Nugget Cafe has country-style food at inexpensive prices and friendly service. For lunch or dinner, also try Pricco's for its great food and cool ambiance. Both are on Main Street.

Ouray should be called the "Hot Springs Capital of Colorado." Three hotels in town—the Best Western Twin Peaks, Box Canyon Lodge, and Weisbaden—have facilities fed by natural hot springs, but locals flock to the pools of varying temperatures from cool to steamy at the Ouray Hot Springs Pool on Hwy. 550 on the northern end of town. Just down the road on Hwy. 550 in Ridgway, the Orvis Hot Springs offers a more rustic soaking environment in a large sand-bottomed pool where bathing suits are optional.

Telluride

No visit to Telluride would be complete without a trip to Baked in Telluride on S. Fir Street, a combination bakery and brew pub that also serves deli sandwiches and pizza by the slice in a very laid-back atmosphere. For an authentic Bavarian experience, lift your beer steins full of Paulaner accompanied by a bratwurst at Leimgruber's Bierstube & Restaurant on W. Pacific Avenue.

Durango

In Durango, the Steamworks at 801 E. 2nd Avenue is the perfect place to grab a beer and a bite in a brew pub with a funky industrial decor. Great pizza and live rock or blues music can be found at Farquahrts at 725 Main Avenue.

Six miles north of Durango just off of Hwy. 550, a family atmosphere dominates the Trimble Hot Springs. An Olympic-sized pool features cooler water, while a soaking pool with jets offers hot-tub-temperature soaks. A green lawn with shade trees and picnic tables make this a nice place for a postrun picnic.

Resources

Accommodations

All the historic towns in this chapter have an abundance of charming bed and breakfasts and outstanding hotels. Because of the hosts' knowledge of local trails and the unique beauty of their accommodations, two standouts include the Chipeta Sun Lodge in Ridgway (800-633-5868) and the River House Bed & Breakfast in Durango (800-254-4775). Otherwise, your best bet is to get full lodging information from the following tourism offices.

Crested Butte Chamber of Commerce Visitor's Center, 601 Elk Avenue, Crested Butte, CO 81224; 970-349-6438 or 800-545-4505; http://-www.cbinteractive.com

Crested Butte Reservations, 800-215-2226 or 800-544-8448

Durango Area Chamber Resort Association, 111 S. Camino del Rio, Box 2587, Durango, CO 81302; 800-525-8855 or 970-247-0312; http://www.durango.org

Ouray Chamber Resort Association, Box 145, Ouray, CO 81427; 800-228-1876 or 970-325-4746

Telluride Visitor's Center, 666 W. Colorado Avenue, Box 653, Telluride, CO 81435; 800-525-3455 or 970-728-4431; http://-www.telluridemm.com

Camping

Often the best views in southwestern Colorado are framed by a tent window. National Forest and Bureau of Land Management land surrounds all the towns, so camping is abundant. You can stay at one of the established campgrounds, some with running water and outhouses, or if you are well prepared, you can revel in the joys of dispersed camping by pulling off a forest service road at a nice spot and pitching a tent. Reservations can be made in advance at many of the area's national forest campgrounds by calling 800-280-CAMP. For more information on other camping opportunities, contact the following offices.

Black Canyon of the Gunnison National Monument, 102 Elk Creek, Gunnison, CO 81230; 970-641-2337

Gunnison Gorge, Bureau of Land Management, 2505 S. Townsend, Montrose, CO 81401; 970-240-5300

National Forest, Ouray Ranger District Office, 2505 S. Townsend, Montrose, CO 81401; 970-240-5300

San Juan National Forest Office, 701 Camino del Rio, Room 101, Durango, CO 81301; 970-247-4874

Taylor River/Cebolla District Forest Service Office, 216 N. Colorado Street, Gunnison, CO 81230; 970-641-0471

Green Lake Loop

—*Scott Boulbol*

A single-track and dirt-road loop just outside Crested Butte that tops out at beautiful Green Lake. The lake is nestled at the base of the sheer rock eastern wall of Mt. Axtell.

Time: 1.25–1.5 hours
Distance: 5.1 miles
Start & End Elevation: 9,260 feet
Total Elevation Gain: 1,620 feet
High Point: 10,720 feet
Low Point: 9,260 feet
Best Season: Midsummer to early fall
Support Points: None
Runability: 90%
Difficulty: Moderate
Type: Lollipop loop
Map: Trails Illustrated Number 133
Contact: Taylor River/Cebolla District Forest Service Office, 970-641-0471

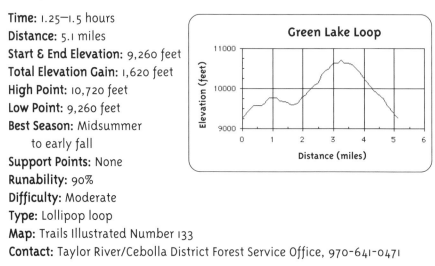

Kirk Apt trains for the Hardrock 100 in his backyard near Crested Butte. Photo by Scott Boulbol.

About the Trail

According to local ultrarunning star Kirk Apt, this is one of the favorite Crested Butte trail runs among locals. When we arrived at Green Lake, we understood why he loves it so much. This trail offers stunning views of the valleys and peaks surrounding Crested Butte. The rewards for the serious climb are plentiful when you reach the turnaround point at Green Lake. The trail meanders through vast aspen groves and dense pine forest, until it reaches huge rock slides below Mt. Axtell. The wildflowers were spectacular when we were there in July, despite an early summer drought. Luckily, Kirk was doing his last training run before his attempt at the Hardrock 100, probably the hardest 100-mile trail race in the country. As a result we were able to keep up with him and even enjoy these views. Kirk placed third overall in the race, so maybe our mellow pace was just what he needed.

Trailhead Access

From Crested Butte, drive west on Kebler Pass Road about 3.5 miles to Wildcat Trail Road, turn left onto the dirt road and park there.

Trail Description

This is a clockwise loop with an out-and-back jaunt to Green Lake in the middle. Follow the Wildcat Trail Road south and east about 1.7 miles as it climbs toward Wildcat Creek. Just before the creek at a sharp left curve in the road, look for a sign nailed to a tree indicating the Green Lake trailhead on the right. Turn right onto the Green Lake Trail and continue to climb about 2 miles all the way up to the lake. Turn around at the lake and head back on the same trail for about 0.5 mile. Look hard for a left-hand turn onto an unmarked intersecting trail (called the Wildcat Trail on maps). This later turns into a four-wheel-drive road that quickly descends down to Coal Creek and the start/finish of the run. On the descent, be sure to stay to the right at each of the intersecting trails. These other trails lead to Coal Creek, west of where your car is parked, so if you find yourself back on Kebler Pass Road, turn right to get back to your car.

Alternative Route

This trail can be done as a longer loop, from downtown Crested Butte, as the locals do it, but it is poorly marked and difficult to follow. At the time of our

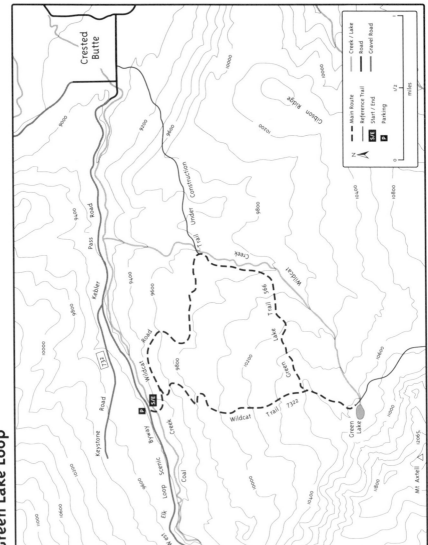

Green Lake Loop

research, the city was planning on up-grading this route, so check the latest maps and talk to the local bike shops.

Trail Notes
- Light traffic
- Dogs must be under voice and sight control at all times
- No facilities
- No potable water
- Bikes allowed
- No fee charged

Junction Creek
(Colorado Trail Southern Terminus)
—Monique Cole

The southern end of the 500-mile Colorado Trail begins as an enjoyable, easy single track along Junction Creek, climbing up to great views of the Durango area.

Time: 1.0–2.0 hours
Distance: 5 miles
Start & End Elevation: 6,560 feet
Total Elevation Gain: 1,640 feet
High Point: 8,202 feet
Low Point: 6,560 feet
Best Season: Late spring
    to early fall
Support Points: None
Runability: 100%
Difficulty: Easy
Type: Out-and-back
Map: Trails Illustrated Number 504
Contact: San Juan National Forest Office, 970-247-4874

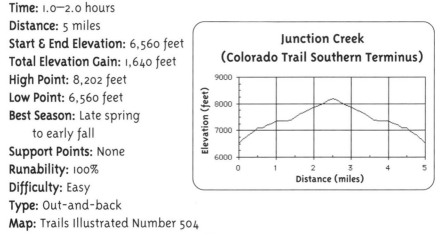

About the Trail

Although this trail is written up as one of the shortest in our book, it could be the beginning of an epic, 500-mile run. Unlike the Colorado Trail's northern terminus—an overtraveled jeep road just south of Denver—its southern end starts as a pleasant trail crisscrossing a creek through ponderosa pine and Gambel oak forests. Along the way, runners will pass some interesting blocks of red sandstone eroded with tiny pockets, caves, and shelves that look like a miniature version of the cliff dwellings in nearby Mesa Verde. After a few miles, the trail crosses the creek on a wide bridge and switchbacks up the west side of the valley, entering a subalpine zone marked by fir and aspen trees. At the top of the hill, you will find a bench at what is called "Gudey's Rest," where you can enjoy views of the red bluffs of Durango and Perins Peak. Mule deer, Abert's squirrels, and rabbits are commonly seen along this popular local trail, and elk can sometimes be spotted in fall and spring. This trail certainly sees its share of mountain bikers, but it is very well maintained and the cyclists are polite about passing runners. Because of its proximity to town, locals flock to this trail after work and on weekend mornings.

Junction Creek (Colorado Trail Southern Terminus)

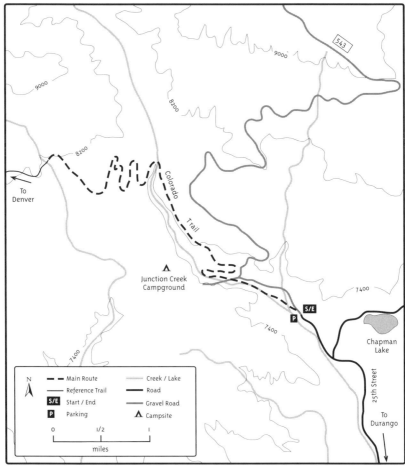

Trailhead Access

From Durango's Main Avenue, head west on 25th Street. After about 3.5 miles, cross a cattle guard marking the boundary of the San Juan National Forest and look for the trailhead and parking area on the left.

Trail Description

This out-and-back route is so well marked, it would be challenging to get lost. From the trailhead, just follow the Colorado Trail signs. After passing the

> ### The "Norm"al Guy Says
> "I'll meet you guys in Denver. Have dinner ready."

access trail to the Junction Creek Campground, the trail rises above the creek, then drops back down and crosses a wide bridge. The climbing gets steeper as the trail ascends the west side of the valley. The switchbacks end at "Gudey's Rest" where you, too, can rest on a bench before turning around and heading back the way you came.

Alternative Route

With enough planning, topo maps, and friends to support you on mountain bikes and four-wheel-drive vehicles, you could theoretically run the Colorado Trail all the way to Denver for a total of about 500 miles.

Trail Notes

- Moderate to high foot and mountain bike traffic
- Horses allowed
- Toilets and potable water at campground
- Dogs must be on a leash or under voice command
- No fee charged

Lizard Head Trail

—Phil Mislinski

A high-altitude single-track run that provides a storybook adventure in the shadow of an impressive 400-foot-tall rock spire.

Time: 3.0–3.5 hours
Distance: 11.2 miles
Start & End Elevation: 10,240 feet
Total Elevation Gain: 3,440 feet
High Point: 12,080 feet
Low Point: 10,040 feet
Best Season: Midsummer
    to early fall
Support Points: None
Runability: 70–90%
Difficulty: Difficult
Type: Out-and-back
Map: Trails Illustrated Number 141
Contact: Telluride Visitor's Center, 800-525-3455, and National Forest, Ouray Ranger District Office, 970-240-5300

Lizard Head Trail — Elevation (feet) vs. Distance (miles)

About the Trail

This run is much like a storybook adventure. It passes through meadows filled with wildflowers, a forest that is right out of a J.R.R. Tolkien book (you may actually see a Hobbit), and high-alpine tundra on the way to a towering rock monolith. The 400-foot-tall Lizard Head rock formation easily provides visions of an evil castle filled with dragons and wizards. This is especially true when seen from afar on a stormy afternoon. If you want to take this run one

Lizard Head Trail

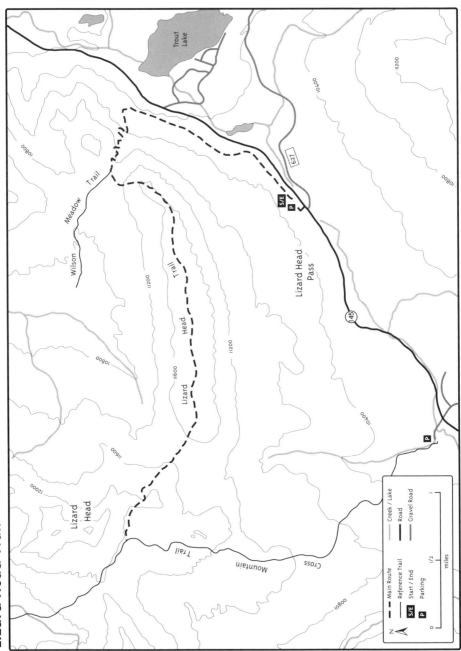

Trout Lake

11200

10400

627

10800

Meadow Trail

S/E
P

Lizard Head Pass

Wilson

11200

Trail

145

Head

10800

11200

Lizard

11600

10400

10800

Lizard Head

11600

12000

P

Trail

Mountain

Cross

10800

N

Main Route
Reference Trail
S/E Start / End
P Parking

Creek / Lake
Road
Gravel Road

0   1/2   1
miles

step further and turn it into a biathlon, Lizard Head has several challenging rock climbing routes. Be sure to consult a local guidebook (Charlie Fowler wrote a few good ones) for climbing route advice because the rock can be bad on some of the routes. Many of the late afternoons bring thunderstorms to this area. Be sure to get an early start.

Trailhead Access

From downtown Telluride take Hwy. 145 west then turn south on Hwy. 145 toward Ophir. Continue on Hwy. 145 approximately 15 miles to Lizard Head Pass. The parking area is on the right at the top of the pass.

Trail Description

From the Lizard Head Pass parking area, head northeast on the single track as it parallels the highway. Follow the trail through the meadow, then turn left on the Wilson Meadow Trail. Enjoy the switchbacks through the forest, then turn left on the Lizard Head Trail. Climb up onto the ridge at 11,600 feet. Enjoy the views of the meadows to the north as you follow the trail west to the base of the monolith. Continue until you reach the intersection with the Cross Mountain Trail (the turnaround point). Return the same way you came in.

Alternative Route

If you need a loop and don't mind running on pavement for a few miles, head

The dark castle of Lizard Head as seen at a distance from the Alta Mine.

The "Norm"al Guy Says

"You guys told me that this was a fairy tale run, but where's the princess waiting to be rescued?"

south on the Cross Mountain Trail from the Lizard Head Trail. Follow this trail until you reach the trailhead at a gravel road just off Hwy. 145. Turn left on the highway and follow it back to the parking area.

Trail Notes

• Light to moderate foot traffic
• Dogs allowed: Voice and sight control at all times and a leash is recommended near the trailhead and parking lot
• Very light horse traffic
• No potable water or toilets at trailhead
• Mountain bikes are not allowed
• No fee charged

Portland/Cascade Falls Loop

—Monique Cole

This trail combines the best of Ouray—mining history, dramatic waterfalls, views of the surrounding peaks—on a gently rolling single-track loop through aspen and pine forests with a steeper out-and-back in the middle.

Time: 1.25–2.5 hours
Distance: 8.4 miles
Start & End Elevation: 8,360 feet
Elevation Gain: 2,180 feet
High Point: 10,080 feet
Low Point: 8,360 feet
Best Season: Summer through fall
Support Points: None
Runability: 95–100%
Difficulty: Easy to moderate
Type: Lollipop loop
Map: Trails Illustrated Number 141
Contact: Ouray Ranger District Office, 970-240-5300

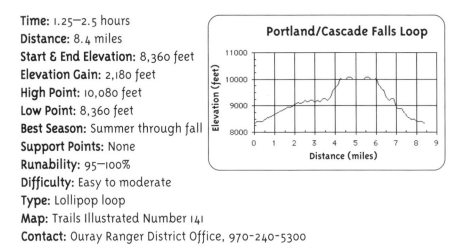

About the Trail

Near Ouray all trails lead straight up a mountain, except for this one. While the stick of the lollipop is a fairly steep switchbacking trail, the candy itself is a gently rolling loop with great vistas of the surrounding San Juans. At the top of the climb, you'll be satisfied by views of Ouray and the spectacular Upper Cascade Falls, where you can dip your feet into a cold pool or just enjoy the fresh scent of pine needles mingling with the mist drifting from the falls. Across the river, the trail continues to the ruins of the Chief Ouray Mine's boardinghouse and machine shop perched precariously on the cliffside. Unfortunately, because it is one of Ouray's gentler trails, the lower loop sees high horse traffic, as evidenced by the odorous piles left behind.

Trailhead Access

From Ouray, head south on Hwy. 550 about a mile and turn left at the sign for the Amphitheater Campground. Veer right at the fork (a left turn takes you to the campground) onto Portland Road and after about 0.25 mile, look for the small parking area on the right and the Portland trailhead across the road.

Trail Description

Follow the trail over a bridge and at the first trail sign, turn right onto the Portland Trail (238) to do the loop

Portland/Cascade Falls Loop

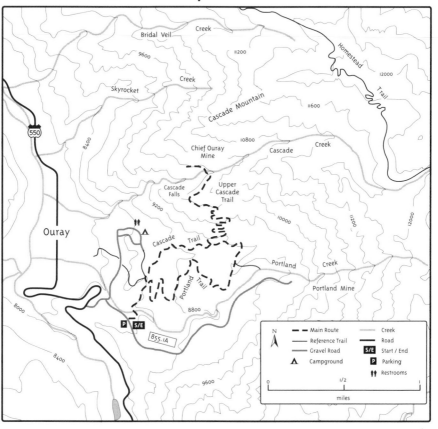

counterclockwise. The trail gradually climbs west with the Portland Creek down below on your right. At the trail sign marking the spur trail to the Portland Mine, take a sharp left, following the main trail toward Upper Cascade Falls. You will pass through some enormous aspen trees as you descend slightly. At the next junction, turn right onto the trail marked as "Chief Ouray Mines" (213—also called Upper Cascade Falls Trail on some maps). After about a dozen switchbacking turns, the trail levels out as it passes under a band of red rock and heads

> ### The "Norm"al Guy Says
> "This route is so beautiful, I almost forgot to count the switchbacks and avoid the horse manure land mines."

north. You'll start to hear the falls before you turn a corner and run the last 100 yards. Here the trail crosses Cascade Creek above the upper falls and continues to the Chief Ouray Mine. There is no bridge and there is a precipitous drop below this dangerous creek crossing—use extreme caution.

For the return, run back the way you came until you reach the junction with the Portland Trail, where you will turn right to close the loop on the Cascade Trail (213). At the Amphitheater Campground access trail, veer left to stay on Trail 213 and follow the signs leading back to the Portland trailhead.

Alternative Route

If you're feeling lazy, skip the trail up to the falls and just do the lower loop for a short, easy romp through the woods with great views of Ouray and the surrounding peaks.

Trail Notes

- Moderate foot traffic
- High horse traffic on lower loop; no horses allowed on Chief Ouray Mine Trail
- Toilets and potable water available at Amphitheater Campground (Memorial Day through Labor Day)

Monique Cole rambles along the Portland Trail above Ouray.

- Dogs must be under voice and sight control; leashes recommended
- No restrictions on mountain bikes (but rules may change soon)
- No fee charged

Summerville Trail

—Scott Boulbol

A smooth and scenic out-and-back run on wide single track near Crested Butte, which can be any length up to about 24 miles (we chose to do about 9.5). Thick aspen groves line the trail, which continually crosses Summerville Creek early and late in the run.

Time: 1.25–2.5 hours
Distance: 9.5 miles
Start & End Elevation: 8,780 feet
Total Elevation Gain: 2,380 feet
High Point: 10,900 feet
Low Point: 8,780 feet
Best Season: Early through late summer
Support Points: None
Runability: 100%
Difficulty: Moderate
Type: Out-and-back
Map: Trails Illustrated Numbers 131 and 132
Contact: Taylor River/Cebolla District Forest Service Office, 970-641-0471

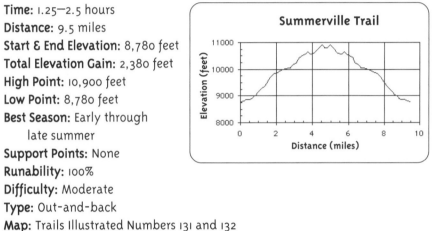

About the Trail

While driving toward Crested Butte in search of trails, we decided to stop for a quick run at the Summerville trailhead. It turned out to be a wonderful run, and made the final fifty for this book. In the first minutes, this trail becomes unforgettable, as it wanders through beautiful aspen groves and back and forth across the creek. The trail is extremely smooth, with few rocks or roots to interfere with your stride. This is a plus as you will find yourself constantly staring at the thick lush flora around the banks of the creek, including innumerable types of wildflowers. During our run we became too fascinated with the beauty of the babbling brook, and wound up sitting in it the hard way. The views are not limited to this, however, and the longer you go, the better they get. The turn-around point in this write-up is the first spot where Fossil Ridge is visible, and it is well worth the effort.

Trailhead Access

From Crested Butte, take 135 south to Almont, and turn left on Forest Road 742 (Taylor River Road). Continue on this road about 13.3 miles through Taylor Canyon and look for the tailhead sign on the right. If you reach

Summerville Trail

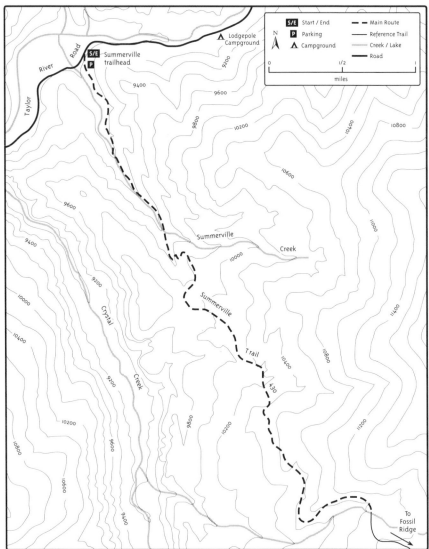

the Lodgepole Campground, you've gone too far.

Trail Description

This is an out-and-back route with no trail intersections, so it is very easy to follow. Simply start south at the Summerville trailhead, and continue until

> ### The "Norm"al Guy Says
> "If I run all the way to Fossil Ridge, I think I may have to lay down for a few million years."

you need to turn back. Our review goes about 4.7 miles out. The trail levels out here for a while, at about 10,860 feet and reaches Crystal Creek. This is the turnaround, and it is also the first place you can see Fossil Ridge to the south and east. Return via the same route.

Alternative Route

For a very long and challenging run, continue on this trail all the way to the ridge. At about 12 miles, you will reach a "T" in the trail, which can be run either east or west along Fossil Ridge. Return via the same route.

Long hours in the saddle have completely destroyed Scott's creek-crossing skills. Photo by Scott Boulbol.

Trail Notes

• Light foot and bike traffic
• Dogs must be on a leash at all times

• No facilities
• No potable water
• No fee charged

Teocalli Ridge Trail

—Scott Boulbol

A narrow and quiet single-track lollipop loop with brutal climbs and crazy descents. Very smooth sandy trail, through thick lush aspen and pine forest, in the shadow of 13,208-foot Mt. Teocalli near Crested Butte.

Time: 2.5–3.5 hours
Distance: 10.4 miles
Start & End Elevation: 9,160 feet
Total Elevation Gain: 3,090 feet
High Point: 11,280 feet
Low Point: 9,120 feet
Best Season: Midsummer
    to early fall
Support Points: None
Runability: 80–90%
Difficulty: Difficult
Type: Lollipop loop
Map: Trails Illustrated Number 131
Contact: Taylor River/Cebolla District Forest Service Office, 970-641-0471

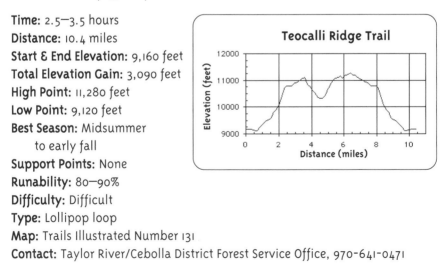

Teocalli Ridge Trail

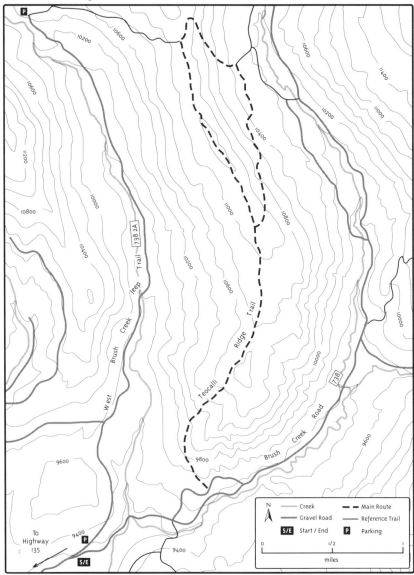

About the Trail

This is one of those dreaded trails that starts making you scream for mommy within the first few miles, rather than leaving that for the last push to the summit. After slowly grinding up to the Teocalli Ridge, the trail then levels off and rolls casually (casually is a relative term in this mountainous terrain) under the towering presence of Mt. Teocalli. After dropping down toward Brush Creek, there is another serious climb, but it is short, and the rest of the way home is downhill. This trail is surprisingly smooth, which makes for some very high-speed descents (we highly recommend riding this on a mountain bike as well), and good sight-seeing even while running. It starts in a sprawling meadow thick with wildflowers and tall grass, and the summit offers panoramic views of snowcapped peaks and high ridge lines. The body of the run takes place among thick groves of aspen, knee-high flora, and dense pines.

Trailhead Access

From Crested Butte, take Hwy. 135 south about 2 miles to the sign for the Crested Butte Country Club where you will turn left onto Brush Creek Road. Start your odometer here. Where the road forks, stay straight on the dirt road. The road here is fairly smooth, but gets rough at the end, so four-wheel drive is recommended. When the odometer reads 5.7 miles, there should be a fork, and a sign that points to West Brush Creek Road on the left fork. Park here to start the run.

Trail Description

From the fork in the road, run east on the lower road (Brush Creek Road) a little more than 1 mile past the major creek crossing, and look for another fork. Stay left here and climb the steep road. Look for the unmarked trail

Dense foliage and aspens along the Teocalli Ridge Trail. Photo by Scott Boulbol.

(Teocalli Ridge Trail) on the left at a sharp right turn in the road, at the crest of a steep section. As is common back here, there are no signs, but the trail is well worn. Take the trail up the side of the mountain and into a thick aspen grove. The climb is intense, and continues for about 1.2 miles (from where the trail begins), until the top of the ridge. At the fork, follow the sign to Brush Creek (a right turn). The trail drops toward the creek, then a left turn at a fork (the right fork is a faint trail that you may miss) will take you climbing back up toward the Teocalli Ridge Trail again. About 0.75 mile should bring you back to the main trail. Turn left on the Teocalli Ridge Trail and continue all the way back to the road. Turn right and descend along the road back to the car.

Alternative Route

If the "hands-and-knees" climb that begins this trail is not what you had in mind and a shuttle car (definitely a four-wheel-drive truck) is available, it can be done as a shorter one-way run. There is still a climb at the start, but it is considerably easier. Have some-one drive you up the West Brush Creek Road to the north trailhead of the Teocalli Ridge Trail where the road deadends. (Then the shuttle car driver should head back down to the Brush Creek Road intersection to pick you up.) Start running up the trail to the east, and climb for about 1.25 miles. Turn right onto the Teocalli Ridge Trail. Continue south to the southern end of the trail, where it intersects with Brush Creek Road. Turn right here and continue to the fork with West Brush Creek Road where your shuttle will hopefully be waiting for you.

Trail Notes
- Light foot and horse traffic
- Dogs must be under voice and sight control
- Mountain bikes allowed (little to no traffic)
- No potable water
- No restrooms
- No fee charged

Ute Trail

—Phil Mislinski

A mostly soft and sometimes sandy single track that takes you into the depths of black-walled Gunnison Gorge and the gold medal trout waters of the Gunnison River. Unlike most of the other runs in the book, this run *starts* with a downhill.

Time: 1.5–2.5 hours
Distance: 9.1 miles
Start & End Elevation: 6,640 feet
Total Elevation Gain: 1,720 feet
High Point: 6,640 feet
Low Point: 5,320 feet
Best Season: Year-round (extremely hot in midsummer)
Support Points: None
Runability: 90–100%
Difficulty: Moderate
Type: Out-and-back
Map: Trails Illustrated Number 245
Contact: Bureau of Land Management, 970-240-5300

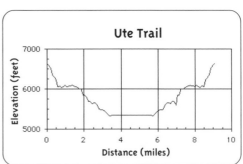

About the Trail

The first half of this run is right out of a Clint Eastwood western flick. A dusty single track takes you through groves of juniper, pinon, and sagebrush where lizards bask on rocks under a hot desert sun. You may find yourself looking for bad guys around every turn as you whistle a tune from *High Plains Drifter* or *The Good, the Bad, and the Ugly*. After cresting a ridge about halfway down the trail, you begin to see the near oasis environment of the Gunnison River. Lush green vegetation lines the waterway and cool breezes can be felt as you enter the river canyon. After a series of steep switchbacks, the trail parallels the river for almost 2 miles as it passes backcountry campsites and a seasonal ranger station in a teepee. Several fishing access trails lead to sandy beaches along the river, which make ideal cooldown sites before the climb back to the parking lot.

Trailhead Access

From Montrose head west on Hwy. 50 for 9.3 miles and turn right on Falcon Road. After 3.8 miles, continue straight onto Peach Valley Road (gravel). After approximately 6.5 miles, turn right onto Ute Road. Continue on Ute Road for 2.5 miles to the parking area. A good four-wheel-drive vehicle is necessary for the upper parts of Ute Road. (See Alternative Route if you don't have a four-wheel-drive vehicle.)

Trail Description

From the parking lot, head east down the marked single track immediately

The Ute Trail enters the oasis along the Gunnison River.

behind the pay slot and bulletin board. Follow the Ute Trail as it winds south then north where it begins to level out. Head east down the steep, rocky switchbacks, then follow the trail south down to the river. The trail ends approximately 0.25 mile past the Ute #1 Campsite. Use any of the fisherman trails down to the river for a swim. Return to your car by retracing your steps.

Alternative Route

If you do not have a four-wheel-drive vehicle that can handle the road to the trailhead, but you can handle an extra 5 miles of running, park at the Ute Road turnoff and start from there. It truly is 2.5 miles from Peach Valley Road to the parking area.

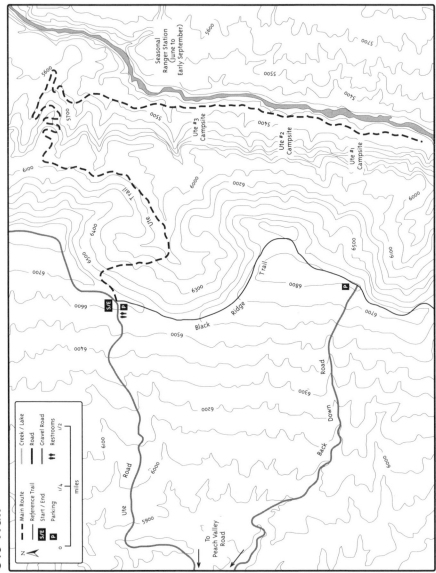

Ute Trail

Trail Notes

- Light to moderate foot traffic
- Dogs allowed: voice and sight control at all times
- Bikes not allowed
- Light horse traffic
- Outhouse but no potable water at trailhead
- Fee charged

Wasatch Trail

—Phil Mislinski

An incredibly scenic run with a steep and burly backcountry experience. This run takes you past several waterfalls as it gets high in the backcountry above Telluride.

Time: 3.5–5.5 hours

Distance: 13.2 miles

Start & End Elevation: 8,760 feet

Total Elevation Gain: 4,480 feet

High Point: 13,140 feet

Low Point: 8,760 feet

Best Season: Late summer to early fall

Support Points: None

Runability: 60–80%

Difficulty: Very difficult

Type: Loop

Map: Trails Illustrated Number 141

Contact: Telluride Visitor's Center, 800-525-3455, and National Forest, Ouray Ranger District Office, 970-240-5300

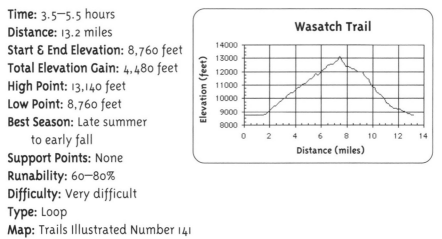

About the Trail

Starting with the relatively mellow Bear Creek Trail, this run can be a bit deceptive. It starts out like many touristy trails with gaggles of hikers and mountain bikers. The number of people on this trail is much like the air pressure—both drop off exponentially with altitude. After passing Bear Creek Falls, the route becomes much more technical, steep, and challenging. That may explain why we didn't see another person until we were on the Bridal Veil Falls Jeep Road a few miles above the falls. We had the area to ourselves for more than 70 percent of the run. This loop is advertised by some of the local bike shops as a great but difficult mountain bike ride. On 90 percent of the Wasatch Trail and the upper sections of the Bridal Veil Falls Jeep Road, a mountain bike is as useful as an old shopping cart filled with bowling balls. Be sure to say "Howdy" if you happen to come across any bikers up high. You will most likely be running right past them.

Trailhead Access

From downtown Telluride, head south on Pine Street until it ends. Cross the creek and follow the short path to the Bear Creek trailhead.

> ### The "Norm"al Guy Says
> "I'll go on the run only if we stop at Baked in Telluride afterward ... and you guys pay."

Trail Description

From the Pine Street trailhead, run south on the Bear Creek Trail. Follow this double-wide trail until Bear Creek Falls comes into view, then turn right onto Wasatch Trail. After climbing the side of the canyon, continue south on Wasatch Trail as it passes Nellie Mine. Stay on the trail to the west of the creek rather than crossing over to pick up the obvious East Fork Bear Creek Trail on the east side. After the Wasatch Trail crosses the creek, veer left at the Gold Hill Trail intersection and follow Wasatch Trail as it winds to the east. (*Note:* The right fork switchbacks up Gold Hill then back around to the Telluride Ski Area.) Continue on Wasatch Trail past the second junction with the East Fork Bear Creek Trail as it follows the East Fork of Bear Creek. Climb to the top of the 13,000-foot pass to the south of Wasatch Mountain. Slide down the snowfield (it is usually still there even in late summer) to pick up the two-rut Bridal Veil Falls Jeep Road. Head north on the Bridal Veil Falls Jeep Road and follow it until you reach the closure gate at Bridal Veil Falls. (*Note:* This two-rut four-wheel-drive road is closed to all motorized traffic and is actually quite fun to run.) After crossing under the closure gate, head down the dirt road, continuing past the bottom of the falls until you reach Hwy. 145. Take this road east back into town.

Alternative Routes

If you have seen Bridal Veil Falls up close and don't want to endure the falls road back to town, you have two other worthwhile options. (1) From the second intersection of Wasatch Trail and East Fork Bear Creek Trail, head north on East Fork Bear Creek Trail and run back down to the Nellie Mine. Return to Pine Street the same way you came in. (2) At the Gold Hill Trail intersection, veer right and take the switchbacks west up Gold Hill. Follow the trail as it turns north then turns into a ski area service road. Take the dirt service road back into town.

The showers are free at the bottom of Bridal Veil Falls.

Wasatch Trail

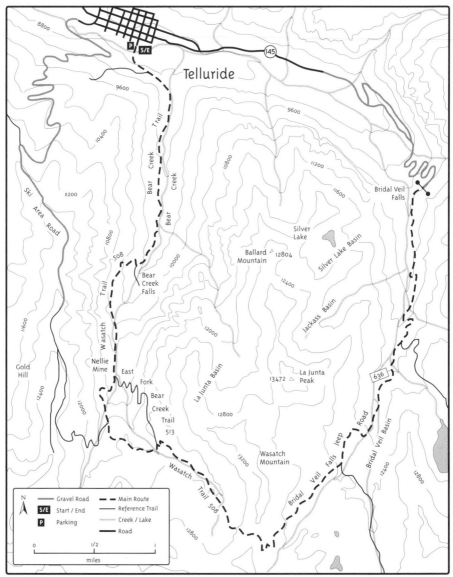

Trail Notes

- Light to moderate foot traffic
- Dogs allowed: voice and sight control at all times and a leash is strongly recommended on the Bridal Veil Falls Jeep Road (from the falls down)
- Light to moderate bike traffic
- Very light horse traffic
- No fee charged

Chapter 13

Grand Junction

Jean-François Lamarque trys Neal's "Quads of Steel" workout program in the Colorado National Monument.

in 1921, the town, the valley, and the mesa retain their "grand" names.

The Colorado flows wide and gentle through Grand Junction, providing calm float trips. Downstream of nearby Loma, though, the rapids and excitement increase through the scenic Ruby and Horsethief Canyons. The Colorado's waters irrigate fertile Grand Valley, which is quickly becoming the Napa Valley of the Rockies. Eleven vineyards are located east of Grand Junction, all with tasting rooms. The wineries are surrounded by fruit orchards where peach, apricot, cherry, and grape trees shade the landscape. Roadside fruit stands are a refreshing stop after a long day running in the surrounding country.

Each spring thousands of Front Range mountain bikers, hikers, and backpackers drive through the town on their way to the canyon country of Moab, Utah, little knowing that the same beautiful slickrock sandstone grandeur exists right near Grand Junction. Just to the south, Colorado National Monument is filled with 32 square miles of natural rock sculptures—massive spires, huge domes, balanced rocks, windows, stone pedestals, and arches.

Part of the greater Colorado Plateau, with Grand Canyon, Bryce Canyon, and Arches as geological kissing cousins, the high country of Colorado National Monument rises 2,000 feet

Perhaps its Western Slope location has kept Grand Junction a relative secret among Colorado's recreational meccas. To the east, Grand Mesa towers a mile over the town. The largest flat-topped mountain in the country has 53 square miles of nearly flat terrain at 10,000 feet in elevation. To the north are the purple-gray Book Cliffs, and the entire county is filled with dinosaur bones.

The town was named for its location at the junction of the Grand and Gunnison Rivers. Although the Grand River was renamed the Colorado River

above the floor of Grand Valley. Over millions of years, wind, water, and frost have slowly carved away at the layers of sandstone, shale, and other sedimentary rocks, creating an unrivaled natural sculpture garden. Iron and other minerals in the rock provide a diverse palette of colors—reds, yellows, purples, and browns.

Neighboring the national monument is the Bureau of Land Management's 72,000-acre Black Ridge Canyon's Wilderness Study Area. The gem of this park is the spectacular Rattlesnake Canyon, home to the world's second highest concentration of natural rock arches. With twelve arches, the largest of which spans 120 feet, it is second only to Arches National Park. But you won't see trains of RVs winding through this land; its rugged, remote location guarantees visitors some solitude.

The semidesert canyon country is home to pinon pines and junipers, ravens, swifts, rock wrens, and jays, desert bighorns, mountain lions, and coyotes. And biting gnats in the summer. Bug repellent should be packed, along with plenty of sunscreen and water. Midsummer afternoon temperatures are scorching, making early morning, spring or fall runs more pleasant.

Après-Run

The buffalo burgers, salads, sandwiches, pizza, pasta, and, of course, fresh-brewed beers at the Rockslide Restaurant and Brewery at 401 Main Street are a happy alternative to Grand Junction's fast-food establishments. Also try Grits along Hwy. 50 for an eclectic breakfast, lunch, or dinner.

Motels are Grand Junction's mainstay; call the Visitor & Convention Bureau at 800-962-2547 for more info. Or stay at one of the bed and breakfasts outside of town like the Mt. Garfield (800-547-9108) or the Stonehaven (800-303-0898).

The Saddlehorn Campground (fee charged) within Colorado National Monument, with running water in the bathrooms, is a plush place to camp. While the eighty sites are first-come, first-serve, they are rarely filled to capacity. Backcountry camping is free, but stop in at the visitor's center for the required permit. There's also plenty of roadside camping opportunities in the Black Ridge WSA. Call the BLM at 970-244-3000 for more information.

Resources

Grand Junction Visitor's Center, 740 Horizon Drive, Grand Junction, CO 81506; 800-962-2547 or 970-244-1480

Colorado National Monument, Fruita, CO 81521-9530; 970-858-3617

Bureau of Land Management, 2815 H Road, Grand Junction, CO 81506; 970-244-3000

Monument Canyon Trail

—Phil Mislinski

A relatively easy, long run on mostly soft, rolling single track with some steep, rocky switchbacks. Amazing views of several of the best rock formations in the monument.

Time: 2.0–3.0 hours
Distance: 11 miles
Start & End Elevation: 4,700 feet
Total Elevation Gain: 1,800 feet
High Point: 6,100 feet
Low Point: 4,700 feet
Best Season: Spring and fall
Support Points: National
    Monument Road
    (turnaround point)
Runability: 98–100%
Difficulty: Easy to moderate
Type: Out-and-back
Map: Trails Illustrated Number 208
Contact: Colorado National Monument, 970-858-3617

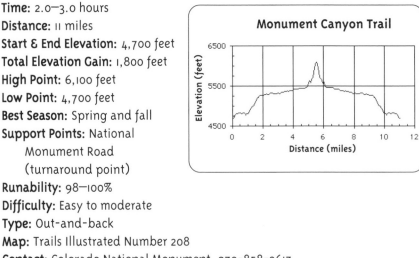

About the Trail

As we made our way up Monument Canyon, the pace continued to get slower and slower. The reduced speed was purely a product of the incredible scenery, not trail difficulty. The trail is moderate to easy for most of its length, with the exception of the top mile. This trail does, however, pass through some of the most breathtaking scenery in Colorado. Along the way you will pass Independence Monument, the Sentinel Spire, Kissing Couple, and Cleopatra's Couch. Each of these rock formations is awe inspiring by itself. Together they are overwhelming. You will want to drag the run out for 2.5 hours or more just so you can take in all the sights.

Trailhead Access

From Grand Junction, head west on I-70 to the Colorado National Monument west entrance (Hwy. 340). The trailhead is located approximately 2 miles southeast of the west entrance on Hwy. 340. The sign along the highway is small, so keep your eyes open.

Trail Description

In the words of our reluctant guide and beer-drinking buddy, Neal, "You follow this trail until you hit the road,

Monument Canyon Trail

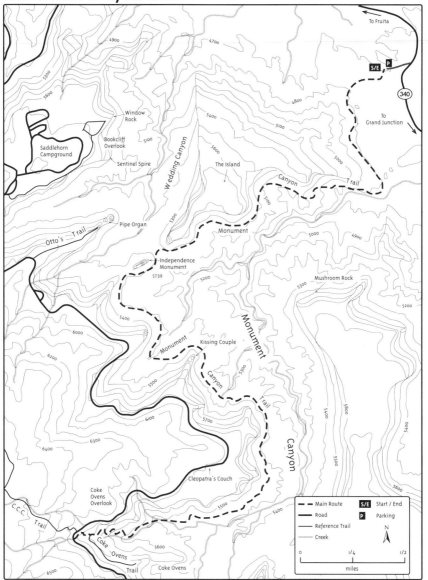

then you turn around and come back. Be careful near the top. If you fall, it's really gonna hurt."

This trail is extremely easy to follow. The trail starts at Hwy. 340 and goes to the National Monument Road.

Follow the obvious trail for as long as you like (or until you hit the road) then turn around and come back. It is a good idea to take two water bottles and some food so you can spend more time enjoying the soft trail and great views.

Alternative Routes

Do this as a long out-and-back or shorten it by turning around earlier. Keep in mind that you will miss some of the incredible scenery if you don't run all the way to the rim. You may also want to do a quick out-and-back on the Coke Ovens Trail when you reach the rim. The views from this trail are great.

Trail Notes
- Light foot traffic
- Dogs are not allowed
- No outhouses or potable water along trail
- Bikes are not allowed
- Very light to no horse traffic
- Hunting is not allowed
- No fee charged

Neal Beidleman demonstrates the proper methods for obtaining "Quads of Steel" on the Monument Canyon Trail.

Rattlesnake Canyon Trail

—*Scott Boulbol*

A high-desert lollipop loop just west of Colorado National Monument. The run culminates with a loop around Rattlesnake Canyon, an area with one of the largest collections of natural rock arches in the world.

Time: 3.0–5.0 hours
Distance: 12.25 miles
Start & End Elevation: 4,645 feet
Total Elevation Gain: 1,615 feet
High Point: 5,710 feet
Low Point: 4,645 feet
Best Season: Spring and fall
Support Points: None
Runability: 80–95%
Difficulty: Moderate
Type: Lollipop loop
Map: Bureau of Land Management
Contact: Bureau of Land Management, 970-244-3000

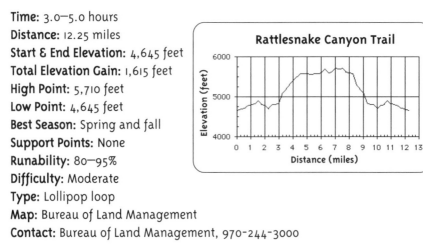

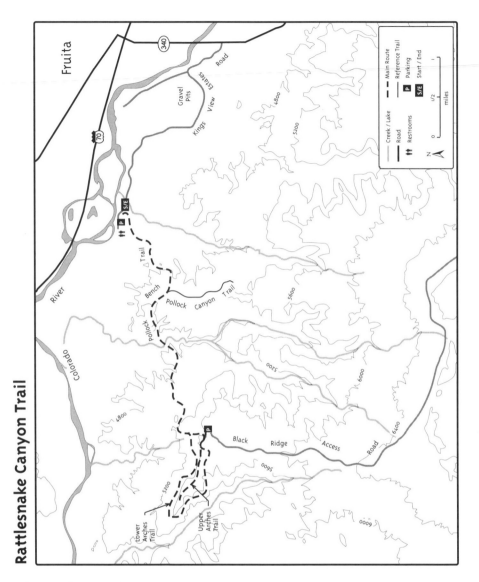

About the Trail

Buzz Burrell, longtime trail explorer and runner, has lived and run just about everywhere in Colorado. When we asked him about some of his favorites in the state, he said that this one was among the best. With Buzz you never quite know what kind of overland pain-fest you are getting into. Much to our delight, this trail lived up to his praises and our expectations. This is a truly breathtaking run through the high desert southwest of Grand Junction. As if the beginning is not great enough, with its roller-coaster romp up and down several canyon walls, the reward truly comes at the short loop called the "Parade of Arches." The trail reaches

> ## The "Norm"al Guy Says
> "Why on earth would we run all this way just to see a bunch of rattle-snakes? This place should be called 'Arches Canyon' instead."

Rattlesnake Canyon after about 7 miles, then follows the rim past more natural arches than we could count. While Rattlesnake Canyon may have fewer total arches than Arches National Park, they are all concentrated into a small, breathtaking area. At every bend in the trail, we looked up to discover another gorgeous arch carved out of the red sandstone.

Trailhead Access

From Grand Junction, head west on I-70, then take the Fruita/Hwy. 340 exit. Take Hwy. 340 southeast 1.5 miles and make a right on Kings View Estates Road toward the Horsethief Canyon State Wildlife Area. Take this road west about 2.5 miles to the Pollock Bench trailhead.

Trail Description

Head south on the Pollock Bench Trail. At the intersection with Pollock Canyon Trail, veer right to stay on Pollock Bench Trail toward Rattlesnake Canyon. The trail will turn west and roll up and down over two canyons for about 5 miles, until it intersects with the Lower Arches Trail. Stay to your right at this intersection. You will be running northwest for about a mile with a ridge to your left. Then the trail makes a U-turn around the end of the ridge and heads southeast. After about another mile, the trail turns left again

One of the many arches along the Rattle-snake Canyon Trail.

and leads directly under Rainbow Arch. After climbing a ridge, turn left on the Upper Arches Trail and continue about 0.5 mile to the trail's end. Re-trace your steps on Upper Arches Trail, but pass left of Rainbow Arch instead of running directly under it. Soon you will reach a connecting trail for the Lower Arches Trail/Pollock Bench Trail; a left turn here brings you over a ridge to the Pollock Bench Trail. Turn right and retrace your steps to the parking area.

Trail Notes
- Light traffic
- Dogs allowed on leash
- Toilets at trailhead
- Bikes allowed on the first part of the Pollock Bench Trail
- No fee charged

Appendix

Colorado Trail Races

Below is a list of trail races in Colorado. Because dates change each year, we have merely listed the trails under the month in which they normally are held. Also, races may cancel, contact phone numbers may change, and routes may alter. An excellent resource for up-to-date race information is the comprehensive calendar printed in *Rocky Mountain Sports* magazine, a free publication distributed throughout Colorado. Call 303-861-9229 for a distribution site near you.

April

Collegiate Peaks 25- and 50-miler
Buena Vista
719-395-6612

May

City of Evergreen Trail Race Series:
Alderfer Three-Sisters Trail Race
6 miles
Evergreen
303-674-6441

June

Horsetooth Mountain Trail Run
8 miles
Fort Collins
970-229-3117

Snow Mountain Ranch Race Series
5K/10K, 25K, 50K
Winter Park
970-887-2152

City of Evergreen Trail Race Series–
Mt. Falcon
5 miles
Evergreen
303-674-6441

Fila Vertical K
3.5 miles
Vail
719-633-9740

U.S. Fila SkyMarathon
and Half-Marathon
Aspen
719-633-9740

July

Vail Hillclimb
7.5 miles (mostly dirt road)
970-479-2280

Hardrock 100
100 miles
Silverton
303-387-5887

Snow Mountain Ranch Race Series
5K/10K, 25K, 50K
Winter Park
970-887-2152

Mosquito Marathon & 15-Miler
Leadville
719-486-2202

Grin and Bear It Trail Run
Crested Butte
970-349-5326

Vail Half Marathon
13.1 miles (mostly dirt road)
970-479-2280

Lake City 50-Mile Trail Race
303-442-6914

Squaw Mountain
7 miles
Evergreen
303-674-6441

Sky Half Marathon
Evergreen
970-262-1603

August
Telluride Get High
29.6 and 15 miles
970-728-1404

Pikes Peak Ascent
13.4 miles
Manitou Springs
719-473-2625

Pikes Peak Marathon
Manitou Springs
719-473-2625
800 participants

Leadville Trail 100
100 miles
719-486-3502 (Send SASE to Box 487, Leadville, CO 80461)

Breckenridge Crest
Mountain Marathon
5 miles, 10 miles, or 24.5 miles
970-453-6422

Fastrek Mountain Series: Saxon Mountain Hill Climb
13 miles
303-567-2679

Colorado Conundrum
28 miles
Crested Butte
970-349-0140

September
Oh-Be-Joyful
23 miles
Crested Butte
970-349-0140

Breckenridge Crest Mountain Races
26.2, 10, and 5 miles
Breckenridge
970-453-6422

Imogene Pass
18 miles
Ouray to Telluride
970-728-9360

Elk Meadow Trail Run
5.6 miles
Evergreen
303-674-6441

City of Evergreen Trail Race Series–Bergen Peak
11.5 miles
Evergreen
303-674-6441

Ute Mountaineer Golden Leaf Mini-Marathon
13.5 miles
Snowmass
970-925-2849

Vail Evergold 10K
970-479-2280

Norwest Kokopelli Trail Marathon/Half-Marathon/50K Ultra
Grand Junction
970-242-7802

Fastrek Mountain Series: Hamlin Scramble
9 miles
303-567-2679

Two Tall Boys
24.1 miles
Leadville
505-662-2397

October
Holy C.O.W. Trail Stampede
10K/5K
Westminster
303-430-2400, ext. 2223

Index

About the Authors

Pictured (from left to right): Scott Boulbol, Sophia Rose Baker-Boulbol, Phil Mislinski, Monique Cole, and Samantha Cole Mislinski.

Phil Mislinski

As one of seven children, Phil Mislinski started running early while chasing and being chased by his siblings. He was born in Wisconsin, grew up in Sioux Falls, South Dakota, and left the Midwest immediately after finishing high school. The great music scene and active lifestyle of Austin, Texas, were a welcome change while he studied at the University of Texas for his bachelor's degree in aerospace engineering.

Throughout his life Phil has participated in various sports, including football, rugby, ski racing, track, bike racing, and beach volleyball. Upon moving to Boulder, Phil discovered the joys of mountain running while earning a master's degree in remote sensing at the University of Colorado. Now he divides his free time between freelance photography, rock climbing, mountain biking, skiing, volleyball, and, of course, trail running. He entered his first trail race, the Basic Boulder Mountain Marathon, shortly after moving to Colorado in 1993. Since then he has done a multitude of trail marathons, usually finishing in the top ten percent. Writing about and photographing trail running was a welcome change from the satellite technical documents he regularly composes as a real-life "rocket scientist."

Monique Cole

The daughter of a big-wave surfer, Monique Cole grew up on the North Shore of Oahu in Hawaii. Her feet rarely touched land during her childhood when she spent most of her free time surfing and snorkeling in her backyard. After serving time in Los Angeles, where she earned a bachelor's degree in English and French literature, Monique escaped to Boulder. There she adapted to her land-locked home by diving into mountain biking, backpacking, rock climbing, and snowboarding. In 1995 she finished second place in the women's mountain bike division of Iditasport, a 160-mile race on Alaska's snow-covered Iditarod Trail. Eschewing her long-held motto, "I only run for buses," she started trail running soon after meeting her now-husband Phil Mislinski. A childhood accident had left her with a leg-length difference of almost an inch, but on rugged mountain trails her asymmetry never caused the pain she had felt in her previous forays into road running. She surprised herself by finishing seventh in her age group in the 13-mile Pike's Peak Ascent, her first running race.

She combines her love of outdoor sports with a career through freelance writing. Her articles have appeared in a number of magazines, including *Mountain Bike, Bike, Skiing, Mountain Sports & Living,* and *Rocky Mountain Sports,* where she served as senior editor for two years. She lives in Boulder with her husband and their daughter, Samantha Cole Mislinski. Their second child is due to arrive in April 1999.

Scott Boulbol

Long before stepping foot in Colorado, Scott Boulbol knew he belonged there. During his childhood in New York, the Rocky Mountains beckoned in his dreams. So after finishing high school, Scott packed up and moved to Boulder where he earned a journalism degree at the University of Colorado. Then he moved to Vail, where he spent six years completing his childhood dream by becoming a ski bum. After two years of television and video production work, he began a long career in the restaurant business, realizing it was a much easier way to support his "outdoor habits." In those days, he explored the mountains on skis and snowshoes in winter, and on a mountain bike in summer.

He met his wife Kathy in Vail in 1989, and the two moved back to Boulder in 1992, where Scott returned to CU for a bachelor's degree in film production. In the relatively balmy Boulder climate he soon fell in love with trail running. While he has finished several Mount Taylor Winter Quadrathlons in New Mexico and hopes to finish an Ironman-length triathlon in 1999, running is his specialty. At both the 1995 and 1996 Pikes Peak Marathons, he finished in under 5 hours and cracked the top 30 in fields of nearly 900 runners. Recognizing that he was slowing down in recent years despite training equally hard, he decided the only answer was to run farther. In the summer of 1998, he finished the brutal Lake City 50-mile run as training for the Leadville Trail 100. A recurring knee injury forced him to quit at the 63-mile mark, but he swears he will return in 1999 for another attempt. He lives in Boulder with his wife, Kathy, their daughter Sophia Rose, and his favorite running buddy, an Australian shepherd named Taz.